Math in Plain English

Literacy Strategies for the Mathematics Classroom

Amy Benjamin

EYE ON EDUCATION

EYE ON EDUCATION
6 DEPOT WAY WEST, SUITE 106
LARCHMONT, NY 10538
(914) 833–0551
(914) 833–0761 fax
www.eyeoneducation.com

Copyright © 2011 Eye On Education, Inc. All Rights Reserved.

For information about permission to reproduce selections from this book, write: Eye On Education, Permissions Dept., Suite 106, 6 Depot Way West, Larchmont, NY 10538.

Sponsoring Editor: Robert Sickles
Production Editor: Lauren Beebe
Copyeditor: Richard Adin, Freelance Editorial Services
Designer & Compositor: Richard Adin, Freelance Editorial Services
Cover Designer: David Strauss

Library of Congress Cataloging-in-Publication Data

Benjamin, Amy, 1951–
  Math in plain English : literacy strategies for the mathematics classroom / Amy Benjamin.
    p. cm.
  ISBN 978-1-59667-186-7
  1. Mathematics—Study and teaching (Elementary) 2. Mathematics—Study and teaching (Middle school) 3. Communication in mathematics. I. Title.
  QA11.2.B46 2011
  510.71′2—dc22
                                                    2011012932

10 9 8 7 6 5 4 3 2

Also Available from EYE ON EDUCATION

**Solving Behavior Problems in Math Class, Grades K–12:
Academic, Learning, Social, and Emotional Empowerment**
Jennifer Taylor-Cox

**Math Intervention:
Building Number Power with Formative Assessments,
Differentiation, and Games, Grades 3–5**
Jennifer Taylor-Cox

**Math Intervention:
Building Number Power with Formative Assessments,
Differentiation, and Games, Grades PreK–2**
Jennifer Taylor-Cox

Family Math Night: Math Standards in Action
Jennifer Taylor-Cox

Family Math Night: Middle School Math Standards in Action
Jennifer Taylor-Cox and Christine Oberdorf

**Mathematics Coaching Handbook:
Working with Teachers to Improve Instruction**
Pia M. Hansen

Engaging Mathematics Students Using Cooperative Learning
John D. Strebe

**Differentiated Instruction for K–8 Math and Science:
Activities and Lesson Plans**
Mary Hamm and Dennis Adams

**Differentiated Assessment in Middle and
High School Mathematics and Science**
Sheryn Spencer Waterman

**Teaching, Learning, and Assessment Together:
Reflective Assessments for Middle and
High School Mathematics and Science**
Arthur K. Ellis and David W. Denton

**Assessing Middle and High School Mathematics and Science:
Differentiating Formative Assessment**
Sheryn Spencer Waterman

**Differentiated Instruction:
A Guide for Elementary School Teachers**
Amy Benjamin

Acknowledgements

Having written this book from the perspective of an English Language Arts specialist, and not a mathematics specialist, I relied on the advice and expertise of several mathematics teachers whom I interviewed. I wish to thank Alison Garber, Jacob Krane, and Melissa McCormand for opening their classrooms to me, allowing me to learn from their excellent rapport with their students. Their ability to make math accessible by having students use the language arts as a means for learning opened my eyes to the possibilities described in this book. I also wish to thank Angelica Diaz, Virginia Newlin, Jessica O'Gorman, and Wendy B. Sanchez for their detailed reviews and commentary. Their insights were both encouraging and enlightening. Also, many thanks to my husband, Howard Benjamin, the official "math person" in the household, who served as a sounding board and translator of my thoughts into plain English.

Finally, I thank Robert N. Sickles and his outstanding staff at Eye On Education for giving me the opportunity to write this book, and Lauren Beebe, who carefully presided over its production details.

Meet the Author

Amy Benjamin taught English for more than thirty years in New York. As a specialist in literacy education, she is a consultant for the National Council of Teachers of English and has worked with educators throughout the United States. Amy has been recognized for excellence in teaching by the New York State English Council, Tufts University, and Union College. Her professional goal is to help teachers in all subject areas to infuse vocabulary, reading comprehension, and writing-to-learn activities into their pedagogy. This is Amy's eleventh book for Eye On Education.

Free Downloads

Select materials in this book are also available on Eye On Education's website as Adobe Acrobat files. Permission is granted to purchasers of this book to download these materials and print them.

You can access these downloads by visiting Eye On Education's website: www.eyeoneducation.com. From the home page, click on FREE, then click on Supplemental Downloads. Alternatively, you can search or browse our website to find this book, then click on "Log in to Access Supplemental Downloads."

Your book-buyer access code is **MPE-7186-7**.

Index of Free Downloads

Figure 1.1. Words with Multiple Meanings	page 11
Figure 3.1. Alpha Board to Elicit Background Knowledge	page 24
Figure 4.1. Venn Diagram	page 51
Figure 4.2. Class Graph 1	page 52
Figure 4.3. Class Graph 2	page 53
Figure 6.1. Graduated Complexity of the Outline Form	page 68
Figure 9.1. Self-Reflection Graphic Organizer	page 89
Figure 9.2. Math Writing Rubric	page 90

Contents

Acknowledgements iv
Meet the Author v
Free Downloads vi
User's Guide xi
Introduction xiii
    Math and Me xxii

Strategy 1 Teaching Mathematical Words Explicitly 1
    Teaching the Words of Mathematics and the
        Academic Words Surrounding Them 2
        Acquisition-Learning Hypothesis 3
        Monitor Hypothesis 4
        Natural Order Hypothesis 5
        Input Theory 6
        Affective Filter Theory 6
    Three Categories of Mathematical Words 7
        Category 1: Words that We Encounter Almost
            Exclusively in Mathematics 7
            Discovering a New Concept that Is Called by a New Word 8
            Refining a Known Concept with a New Word 9
            Naming a Known Concept with a New Word 9
        Category 2: Words with Multiple Meanings Outside
            of the World of Mathematics 10
        Category 3: Phrases of Mathematics 11
    Numbers and Counting 12
    Conclusion 14

Strategy 2 Teaching Academic Words Implicitly 15
    What Can Be Done to Bridge the Vocabulary Gap? 16
    Conclusion 20

**Strategy 3 Reinforcing Reading Comprehension
Skills that Apply to Mathematics** 21
    What We Mean by "Teaching Reading in the Content Areas" 21
    Before Reading: Connect! 22
        Connection 1: Background Knowledge and Key Vocabulary 22
        Connection 2: Establish a Purpose for Reading 26

      Connection 3: Think About the Genre (Establish Expectations) 27
          Zigzag Reading 27
      Connection 4: Overview 28
  During Reading: Concentrate! 28
  After Reading: Communicate! 29
      Outlining to Communicate Understanding of Text 29
      Paraphrasing: Reword and Regroup 30
  What Kinds of Reading? 31
      Reading Explanations in the Mathematics Textbook 31
      Getting to Know the Textbook: The Table of Contents 32
      Do the Math on the Table of Contents 35
      Chapter Overviews 36
  Three Gears of Prereading: Skimming, Scanning, Sampling 36
  Reading the Explanations in the Mathematics Textbooks: 37
  Achieving Speed and Accuracy as a Reader of Mathematics 37
      Speed 37
      Accuracy 38
      Vocabulary and Cultural Knowledge 39
  Conclusion 40

Strategy 4 Teaching Mathematics with Metaphor and Gesture 41
  Analyzing Well-Known Math Metaphors 45
  The Math-as-Motion Metaphor 47
  Using Gestures to Clarify Metaphors and Meaning 47
  Graphic Representations as Metaphor 49
  Conclusion 53

Strategy 5 Unlocking the Meaning of Word Problems 55
  Background Knowledge and Mathematical Problems 57
  When Working with Students Individually 60
  A Cooperative Learning Strategy for Creating,
      Solving, and Evaluating Word Problems 60
  Conclusion 61

Strategy 6 Teaching Note-Taking Skills for Mathematics 63
  Three *As* of Math Note Taking 64
  Note Taking as a Meaning-Making Activity 65
  Math and Me 70
  Conclusion 71

Strategy 7 Using Language-Based Formative
Assessment in Mathematics 73
  Questions and Classroom Dialogue 75

    Changing the Feedback Game: Numbers or Comments? 76
    How Teachers Can Use Language Modes to Assess Learning 78
    Conclusion 80

Strategy 8 Connecting Memorization to Meaning in Mathematics ... 81
    Math, Mental Math, and Memorization 81
    Memorizing Tables and Sequences 82
    Memorizing Definitions vs. Knowing What Something Is 84
    Conclusions 86

Strategy 9 Incorporating Writing-to-Learn Activities in Mathematics 87
    What Kinds of Writing Work Best for Mathematics Learners? 87
    Reasons for *Not* Including Writing in Mathematics 88
        Lack of Skill in Teaching and Responding to Student Writing 89
        Lack of Class Time to Devote to Student Writing 90
        Strong Beliefs About Traditional Mathematics Instruction 91
        Short Writing Assignments: A Model 91
    Four Types of Writing-to-Learn Mathematics 92
    Conclusion 94

Strategy 10 Preparing Students for Algebraic Thinking 95
    Linking Algebra to Grammar 96
    Linking Algebra to a Lesson in Nutrition 98
    Linking Algebra to a Workout at the Gym 98
    Conclusion 99

Appendix 1 Word Components Commonly Seen in Math Language: Or…Words Have Cousins? 101
    The Prefixes 102
    The Combining Forms 105
    The Suffixes 108
    The Roots 109

Appendix 2 Making Connections in Vocabulary 111

Works Cited 115

User's Guide

This book is about strategies for using the four modes of language—reading, writing, listening, and speaking—to facilitate and enrich the teaching of mathematics. Although these strategies will work for teaching mathematics at any level, most of the examples and specific references to content focus on third through ninth grades.

The Introduction gives a rationale for creating language-rich mathematics classroom in plain English. This rationale is supported by the Common Core State Standards in Mathematics. These CCSSM consist of eight Standards, each of which depends, to an extent, on the teacher's skillful use of language in the classroom. By language in the classroom, I do not mean the teacher's language alone. The thesis of this book is that students—especially those whose preferred learning style is verbal—need to talk and write their ways into understanding. Verbal learners need to speak, read, write, and listen to each other to internalize the mathematics they are expected to learn.

Most of this book consists of a detailed explanation of ten classroom-ready strategies for incorporating plain English language activities in a mathematics class. I expect you to find that you are already using at least some of these strategies to some extent. I'm hoping that you will embrace and refine more of them in your repertoire of teaching skills.

The two appendices offer useful lists about word components and word connectedness. These lists are not to be served up as gobs of information to be memorized by rote. Rather, they are offered to enrich your own explanations about how the words of mathematics are connected to familiar words in students' vocabularies and lives.

The polarization of mathematics and the language arts is false and unnecessary. The flip side of the "I'm no good in math" coin should not be "But I'm good in English." Being good in English is an advantage that can be leveraged to become good in mathematics. Please read this book with those language-loving learners in mind. Make them believe that mathematical language can become plain English to them.

Introduction

According to Heidi Hayes Jacobs, "Language capacity is at the root of all student performance" (2006, p. 3). Jacobs further notes that listening and reading are receptive language modes, whereas speech and writing are productive language.

By *language capacity*, we mean the ability to receive and interpret language (listening and reading) and to produce language (speech and writing). The language of math, being so specific and often unfamiliar, must become comprehensible if the instruction is to be meaningful. Productive language modes develop after, and as a result of, receptive ones. Therefore, it is essential that the receptive language that students experience in school—the listening and reading that they do—be rich enough to cultivate the speech and writing that students need to do to process, remember, demonstrate, communicate about, and retain what they've learned.

When too much of math learning is passive—that is, when math becomes a spectator sport rather than an active, communicative experience—many students never learn math in a meaningful way. They learn to memorize and deliver what they've memorized on a test. Shallow learning like that is soon forgotten. In the language-rich math classroom that I describe in this book, students engage all four language modes to make sense of math and therefore to find it meaningful and memorable.

As I write this, the state education departments in California, Nevada, Utah, Arizona, Colorado, Wyoming, Oklahoma, Iowa, Illinois, Missouri, Arkansas, Louisiana, Mississippi, Tennessee, Kentucky, Indiana, Florida, Wisconsin, Michigan, North Carolina, South Carolina, Georgia, Ohio, Virginia, West Virginia, Maryland, Hawaii, Massachusetts, New Jersey, Connecticut, New Hampshire, Pennsylvania, and New York have adopted the Common Core State Standards (CCSS) Initiative (2010). According to its Mission Statement,

> The Common Core State Standards provide a consistent, clear understanding of what students are expected to learn, so teachers and parents know what they need to do to help them. The standards are designed to be robust and relevant to the real world, reflecting the knowledge and skills that our young people need fur success in college and careers. With American students fully prepared for the future, our communities will be best positioned to compete successfully in the global economy.

Let's look at the Standards for Mathematical Practice (2010) and consider how they rely upon a language-rich classroom. I'll show each Standard verbatim from the Common Core State Standards for Mathematics document, and then step back and consider it in terms of the language that students must engage in to meet each Standard:

The Standards for Mathematical Practice are framed in terms of what people who are mathematically proficient actually *do and think*:

> **Standard 1: Make sense of problems and persevere in solving them.**
>
> Mathematically proficient students start by explaining to themselves the meaning of a problem and looking for entry points to its solution. They analyze givens, constraints, relationships, and goals. They make conjectures about the form and meaning of the solution and plan a solution pathway rather than simply jumping into a solution attempts. They consider analogous problems, and try special cases and simpler forms of the original problem in order to gain insight into its solution. They monitor and evaluate their progress and change course if necessary. Older students might, depending on the context of the problem, transform algebraic expressions or change the viewing window on their graphing calculator to get the information they need. Mathematically proficient students can explain correspondences between equations, verbal descriptions, tables, and graphs or draw diagrams of important features and relationships, graph data, and search for regularity of trends. Younger students might rely on using concrete objects or pictures to help conceptualize and solve a problem. Mathematically proficient students check their answers to problems using a different method, and they continually ask themselves, "Does this make sense?" They can understand the approaches of others to solving complex problems and identify correspondences between different approaches.

I encapsulate Standard 1 as "The Math Monologue." This Standard is all about self-talk: We want to equip students with the internal math monologue rich enough to guide them through the problem and any obstacles they may encounter. In this internal monologue, the student needs to be asking:

- What is this problem asking me to do? What are the key factors of it (givens, constraints, relationships, goals)? What's my tentative plan?

- What other problems are like this one? How can I simplify? Does my plan seem to be working? If not, what else might I try? At what point did my plan stop working?

- What models can I use to express how my plan for solving this problem is developing?
- How do I use a different method to check my answer?
- Does my answer make sense?

What Standard 1 is asking of the teacher, then, is: "How can you nurture the students' ability to create this internal math monologue? What vocabulary and sequences of questions and answers must the students have?" Students are novices at running an internal math monologue. Teachers need to model their own thinking through a problem, but having students listen is not enough: We have to build in copious opportunities for math conversations in class.

> **Standard 2: Reason abstractly and quantitatively.**
>
> Mathematically proficient students make sense of quantities and their relationships in problem situations. They bring two complementary abilities to bear on problems involving quantitative relationships: The ability to *decontextualize*—to abstract a given situation and represent it symbolically and manipulate the representing symbols as if they have a life of their own, without necessarily attending to their referents—and the ability to *contextualize*—to pause as needed during the manipulation process in order to probe into the referents for the symbols involved. Quantitative reasoning entails habits of creating a coherent representation of the problem at hand; considering the units involved; attending to the meaning of quantities, not just how to compute them; and knowing and flexibly using different properties of operations and objects.

Standard 2 has to do with translations back and forth from the concrete world into the world of mathematics (where quantities and relations are expressed symbolically) and then back into the concrete world. Students need to expand their language to include the symbols of math. They need to use language to go back and forth between the concrete world and the symbolic world of mathematics.

> **Standard 3: Construct viable arguments
> and critique the reasoning of others.**
>
> Mathematically proficient students understand and use stated assumptions, definitions, and previously established results in constructing arguments. They make conjectures and build a logical progression of statements to explore the truth of their conjectures. They are able to analyze situations by breaking them into cases, and can recognize and use counterexamples. They justify their conclusions, communicate them to others, and respond to the arguments of others. They reason inductively about data, making plausible arguments that take into account the context from which the data arose. Mathematically proficient students are also able to compare the effectiveness of two plausible arguments, distinguish correct logic or reasoning from that which is flawed, and—if there is a flaw in an argument—explain what it is. Elementary students can construct arguments using concrete referents such as objects, drawings, diagrams, and actions. Such arguments can make sense and be correct, even though they are not generalized or made formal until later grades. Later, students learn to determine domains to which an argument applies. Students at all grades can listen or read the arguments of others, decide whether they make sense, and ask useful questions to clarify or improve the arguments.

This Standard is all about communication, both receptive and expressive. But communication in mathematics calls for technical definitions of words that are used more broadly in ordinary conversation. The word *argument* itself, for example, does not mean what a child thinks it means. An essential part of becoming a mathematical thinker and doer is teasing out the "math world" definitions from their vernacular definitions. If teachers do not carefully attend to what students think words mean in a mathematical context, we have serious gaps in understanding.

Standard 3 also calls for language that makes comparison possible and to explain flawed reasoning. Conjunctions and conjunctive adverbs such as *but, so, even though, although, because, therefore* are necessary to justify arguments and to explain flawed reasoning, but students don't always know how to marshal these words to bring about mathematical communication. This Standard dovetails perfectly with grammar: In their English Language Arts classes, students should be learning how to join ideas into compound and complex sentences by using conjunctions, conjunctive adverbs, and relative pronouns. (Whether or not they do learn these skills is another matter and is addressed by the English Language Arts CCSS.)

> **Standard 4: Model with mathematics.**
>
> Mathematically proficient students can apply the mathematics they know to solve problems arising in everyday life, society, and the workplace. In early grades, this might be as simple as writing an addition equation to describe a situation. In middle grades, a student might apply proportional reasoning to plan a school event or analyze a problem in the community. By high school, a student might use geometry to solve a design problem or use a function to describe how one quantity of interest depends on another. Mathematically proficient students who can apply what they know are comfortable making assumptions and approximations to simplify a complicated situation, realizing that these may need revision later. They are able to identify important quantities in a practical situation and map their relationships using such tools as diagrams, two-way tables, graphs, flowcharts, and formulas. They can analyze those relationships mathematically to draw conclusions. They routinely interpret their mathematical results in the context of the situation and reflect on whether the results make sense, possibly improving the model if it has not served its purpose.

Here again, as with Standards 1 and 2, students are required to go from real-life situations and the language that describes them to mathematical models, and back again. They use *language* (self-talk or communicating with others) to work through the process of creating their mathematical models and to explain and justify them.

> **Standard 5: Use appropriate tools strategically.**
>
> Mathematically proficient students consider the available tools when solving a mathematical problem. These tools might include pencil and paper, concrete models, a ruler, a protractor, a calculator, a spreadsheet, a computer algebra system, a statistical package, or dynamic geometry software. Proficient students are sufficiently familiar with tools appropriate for their grade or course to make sound decisions about when each of these tools might be helpful, recognizing both the insight to be gained and their limitations. For example, mathematically proficient high school students analyze graphs of functions and solutions generated using a graphing calculator. They detect possible errors by strategically using estimation and other mathematical knowledge. When making mathematical models, they know that technology can enable them to visualize the results of varying assumptions, explore consequences, and compare predictions with data. Mathematically proficient students at various grade levels are able to identify relevant external mathematical resource, such as digital content located on a website, and use them to pose or solve problems. They are able to use technological tools to explore and deepened their understanding of concepts.

Standard 5 calls for a set of general academic words that delineate models: *represent, stand for, symbolize, trend, illustrate.* Each kind of mathematical model (graph, table, equation, flowchart, formula, diagram, etc.) has its own set of vocabulary.

> **Standard 6: Attend to precision.**
>
> Mathematically proficient students try to communicate precisely to others. They try to use clear definitions in discussion with others and in their own reasoning. They state the meaning of the symbols they choose, including using the equal sign consistently and appropriately. They are careful about specifying units of measure, and labeling axes to clarify the correspondence with quantities in a problem. They calculate accurately and efficiently, express numerical answers with a degree of precision appropriate for the problem context. In the elementary grades, students give carefully formulated explanations to each other. By the time they reach high school they have learned to examine claims and make explicit use of definitions.

Although the title of Standard 6 centers on precision, the explanation of it centers on communication. I encapsulate it by saying that Standard 6 is all about developing the habit of using precise terminology and symbols within the world of mathematics. This Standard relates to the condition that many words in the mathematics have looser definitions when used in ordinary—or even in academic—discourse. Obviously, there is a close relationship between accuracy of language and symbols and accuracy of mathematical reasoning.

> **Standard 7: Look for and make use of structure.**
>
> Mathematically proficient students look closely to discern a pattern of structure. Young students, for example, might notice that three and seven more is the same amount as seven and three more, or they may sort a collection of shapes according to how many sides the shapes have.... They recognize the significance of an existing line in a geometric figure and can use the strategy of drawing an auxiliary line for solving problems. They also can step back for an overview and shift perspective. They can see complicated things, such as some algebraic expressions, as single objects or as being composed of several objects....

Pattern-finding and noticing trends are essential in mathematics. We have to recognize, however, that having the language of patterns and trends allows us to notice them in the first place. When we lack the language to name something, that thing can go unnoticed. This concept goes deep into the purpose of language in the human brain: Knowing a word allows us to do more than communicate. Knowing a word allows us to see the borders around a concept and to access that concept and all that is inside it.

So, as "mathematically proficient students look closely to discern a pattern of structure," they do need the vocabulary to name those patterns of structure, lest the patterns be overlooked: Yes, we tend to overlook things for which we have no name!

No name? No notice!

Standard 7 alludes to unitizing—grouping—seeing multiple elements as a unit. Again, having a *name* for the unit facilitates grouping.

> **Standard 8: Look for and express regularity in repeated reasoning.**
>
> Mathematically proficient students notice if calculations are repeated, and look both for general methods and for shortcuts. Upper elementary students might notice when dividing 25 by 11 that they are repeating the same calculations over and over again, and conclude they have a repeating decimal. By paying attention to the calculation of slope as they repeatedly check whether points are on the line through (1,2) with slope 3, middle school students might abstract the equation $(y-2)/(x-1) = 3$. Noticing the regularity in the way terms cancel when expanding general formula for the sum of a geometric series. As they work to solve a problem, mathematically proficient students maintain oversight of the process, while attending to the details. They continually evaluate the reasonableness of their intermediate results.

There is a set of words that facilitates thinking about regularity and repetition, the concepts expressed in Standard 8. Some such words are *repeat, conform, follow, rule, correspond, match, accept*. Students need to use the verb form to help them express what they notice about emergent patterns of regularity that they observe.

So why is a language-rich math classroom essential? Language is essential for making meaning out of the abstract mathematical concepts described in the Common Core State Standards. This book is about aligning classroom experiences involving language-to-learn-math with the CCSS. I've organized it around ten strategies. Whereas the Standards are framed in language about what the mathematically proficient *students* do, I've framed my strategies in language about what the excellent *teachers* of mathematics do:

- *Strategy 1:* Excellent math teachers teach math-related words *explicitly*. They understand that etymology illuminates meaning and they help students make connections between strange-sounding mathematical words (polygon, trinomial) and familiar words (tricycle), as well as words that students learn (or will learn) in other disciplines (polytheism). Learning about how words are related through etymology is a fascinating life-long pursuit that excellent math teachers eagerly embrace.

- *Strategy 2:* Excellent math teachers teach academic words *implicitly*. They enrich their students' receptive vocabulary every day by elevating their vocabulary with just enough familiar context that students can unconsciously figure out the meaning of academic-type words.

- *Strategy 3:* Excellent math teachers reinforce reading comprehension as it applies to math-related text. They understand that reading math is not like reading a story or a poem. (Actually, it's more like reading a poem than one might think, as reading poetry involves a "work-through" not a "walk-through.")

- *Strategy 4:* Excellent math teachers use imagery and metaphor to concretize abstract mathematical concepts. Metaphor—explaining one thing in terms of another—is simultaneously one of the most basic and most sophisticated ways of thinking. Metaphors are almost always visual. When metaphors and imagery are accompanied with gesture, the depth of learning and durability of memory are strengthened.

- *Strategy 5:* Excellent math teachers give strategies for unlocking the secrets of word problems. Actually, there are no "secrets" of word problems. Word problems must be read carefully. But many students have been led astray by unreliable shortcuts.

- *Strategy 6:* Excellent math teachers teach note-taking skills relevant to mathematical comprehension. They understand that note taking reinforces math learning, but it is more than just copying from the board. A student's notes are a window to her thinking, forming those mental footprints on paper that break math down.

- *Strategy 7:* Excellent math teachers use language-based formative assessment. Formative assessment is "along the way" information that helps teachers make decisions: *Are students understanding? Where does their understanding break down? Is my pacing right? Do I need to differentiate?* By just seeing students' answers, teachers can't analyze student needs. With formative assessment that has the student explain their knowledge in *words*, teachers can make better decisions that affect instruction.

- *Strategy 8:* Excellent math teachers know that memorization must be connected to meaning. There will always be controversy about the value of memorization. On one side are those who take for granted that math facts (multiplication tables, single-digit addition and subtraction facts), definitions, and formulas must be memorized. On the other side are the constructivists, who reject rote memorization in favor of discovery learning, which they claim is more durable. In this chapter, I propose a blended approach, where the teachers help the students use language to connect meaning to memorized information.

- *Strategy 9:* Excellent math teachers incorporate writing both as a means to learn and for assessments. Writing does more than express what we already know: Writing causes learning. By writing, we create, transform, mobilize, integrate, and secure what might otherwise be fragile knowledge. Writing whips learning into shape!

- *Strategy 10:* Excellent math teachers prepare students for algebraic thinking. Beginning in the elementary grades, even the primary grades, students should learn the rudiments of algebraic thinking. A student's success in Algebra I is considered a predictor of whether that student will graduate from high school.

I've tied these strategies to the Core Content State Standards in English Language Arts and to English Language Arts content areas. It is only by strengthening interdisciplinary connections that deep and durable learning will evolve. Math is not some isolated, hermetically sealed subject disconnected from other learning throughout the student's day. Particularly in math class, students don't see the relevance, as revealed in the question: "When am I ever going to use this?" The appropriate response is neither the evasive "You never know" nor "You'll use it next year," but is "You'll use it every time you need to be smart because learning math causes you to think and thinking makes you smarter!"

Math and Me

In the course of researching and writing this book, I've unearthed a lot of memories—most of them painful, but with one brief shining moment—about my own experience as a struggling math learner and my experience in turning math language into plain English. Some people become teachers because school fits right into their comfort zone. Having been successful as students, they choose a teaching career, looking to offer new generations of students what they themselves so loved. Teachers often report that they so admired one or more of their own teachers that they sought to do for others what that beloved teacher did for them.

That is not my story. School was a disconcerting, anxiety-producing place for me. I never had a teacher whom I wanted to emulate. I struggled, especially with math. Why I chose to return to the scene of so many years of mortification—classrooms and schools—has to do with issues having nothing to do with this particular book—and it's a story that I may someday explore. For now, let's just say that whatever strengths I ended up having as a teacher stemmed not from my strengths as a student, but from my weaknesses. I understand what it means to "not get it," especially in math class. I dreaded math, considered myself dumb because of it, froze up on tests, was bored beyond endurance in class.

I've always loved language. But the connections between language—reading, writing, vocabulary—were never made plain to me. For example, I happened to have been great at diagramming sentences (and pretty much all things grammar). My lifelong passion for words never found a place in math class. I depended on words to light my way, but the words and symbols of math left me in darkness.

My best friend Lauren was a lot smarter in school than I was. She, like my other friends, sped along an accelerated path, which involved taking geometry in ninth grade, whereas the general population (me) would take it in the tenth. In the state of New York, state-administered tests are famously known as The Regents Exams, "The Regents" for short. Well, despite her academic talents and easy ride through school, Lauren astonished the world by committing the unthinkable at the end of ninth grade: *Lauren failed the geometry Regents!*

Prior to this disaster, Lauren's idea of failure was getting an 89. Lauren was simply not a person who failed anything in school, much less a Regents, much less a Regents in math. It was a hideous twist of fate. One that humiliated Lauren, of course, but one that left me in utter despair. If Lauren could fail the geometry Regents—what chance did I have?

Lauren's disaster loomed large for me throughout my tenth grade geometry experience. Every day, as I sank deeper into the quicksand of proofs, polygons, and principles, I felt overwhelmed and almost hopeless.

Keyword there: *almost* (hopeless). Not that my teacher—who, as I recall, thought a lot more about his job as a coach than his job as a math teacher—ever gave me reason for encouragement. He was nice enough to "pass me" every quarter when my test scores surely didn't merit it. I think that was in acknowledgement of my faithful appearance at "extra help" sessions. Not that they helped much. But there must have been *something*—some hope against hope—in me that got me studying—really *studying*—actually studying—for the inevitable: my nemesis—the Geometry Regents!

And so in April, two months in advance, I began. Every night, I would dip into the "review book," a collection of past Regents Exams with answers and brief explanations of them. I would simply do some questions, check them, go back and do the ones that I got wrong again. After that, I jotted down the explanations of my wrong answers—what I had been thinking, and what I should have been thinking. I worked. I read. I wrote. I worked. I read. I wrote. Two months.

My geometry Regents exam took place forty-three years ago, as I write this. Forty-three years ago! Yet I remember exactly where I sat to take it (by the window, three seats back). I remember exactly how I felt (terrified, but convinced that there could be nothing on that test to surprise me, certainly convinced that I had done my level best to prepare for this day). I remember the words running in my head (Lauren failed this! Lauren failed this! Who are you kidding?). And I remember that something happened that day that had never happened to me before on a math test: I finished early. Very early. I could have knitted a sweater and sewn it together with the time I had left over.

I also remember my score: 90. I got a 90 on the Geometry Regents.

Thereafter, I never gave much thought to formal geometry. Never did another proof. Never transformed another matrix. Never squared another hypotenuse. But what I learned in tenth grade geometry has stayed with me my entire life: I learned how to study. Studying has to be done over time, with a routine, and you have to be doing something, not just looking at something. I learned that I can't just read to study because words I read fly right out of my head. For me to keep the words, I have to write as well as read. I learned that the unfamiliar language of geometry could become familiar. I learned that I could learn.

STRATEGY 1

Teaching Mathematical Words Explicitly

Excellent teachers of mathematics use plain English to teach the words of mathematics *explicitly*. They understand that etymology illuminates meaning. They help students make connections between strange-sounding mathematical words (*polygon, trinomial, denominator*) and familiar words (*tricycle*), as well as words that students learn (or will learn) in other disciplines (*polytheism*). Learning about how words are related through etymology is a fascinating life-long pursuit that excellent teachers of mathematics include in their explanations about terminology.

When I ask mathematics teachers what the biggest stumbling block is in "reading the math," they invariably reply that it is vocabulary. The words of mathematics tend to be long, unfamiliar sounding, and unfamiliar to look at—that is, having letters that are rare in conversational vocabulary: a lot of x, y, z, and strange consonant combinations: *rh, ph, gn*. The sheer unfamiliarity of the appearance of the "math words," combined with the daunting length of the words creates a stumbling block between the reader and the text.

In what we will call ordinary text (as opposed to technical mathematical language), unfamiliar words are often nestled in enough context that the reader can figure out the meaning, if not on the first exposure, then perhaps through subsequent exposures. With mathematical terminology, the words cannot be figured out through contextual clues. Chances are, the new words are introduced with explicit definitions at the outset of a chapter. After that, you're on your own. "We told you once what congruent angles are, now here's a bunch of congruent angles that go about having all kinds of adventures and getting into all kinds of scrapes and problems that you have to figure out."

Many mathematical terms have more than one personality. Words like *value, property, associate, solve,* and even *find* are used broadly in conversation, but very narrowly in the world of mathematics. It's as if they have a "home" personality, which the student knows, but then they adopt a whole new personality when they go to work for math. For math, they suit up and put on a math "game face." This math game face does bear a resemblance to the familiar, conversational meaning, but not all students can deepen their understanding of a mathematical term by connecting it to its vernacular meaning. We must teach students to make these connections if we want them to understand mathematical terms on a deeper level.

Unfortunately, many teachers, in their desire to get students to use mathematical terms precisely, deny that the conversational meaning altogether! "Forget what you think you know about the word *ray* (or *value, property, area, square*, etc.). It doesn't mean what you think it means. In mathematics, it means something different." The problem with this approach is that it strips the student of the most valuable resource for learning that she has: *background knowledge*. The better strategy is to acknowledge and draw from background knowledge about words, open the door to connectedness, and then narrow the word from its familiar meaning to its mathematical meaning in a way that integrates the mathematical meaning into the student's schema. (Appendix 1, page 101, gives detailed etymology that will help you illuminate these connections.)

Then, there are those mathematical phrases that need to be treated as single words. The student needs to process phrases like *base ten system*, *side of an angle*, and *greatest common factor* as units—immediately recognizable codes in the language of mathematics.

The words of mathematics, then, fall roughly into three categories:

- *Mathematics only:* Words that we are likely to encounter only in the world of mathematics: *milligram, frustum, radian, rhombus, quotient,* etc.

- *Multiple meaning:* Words that have a specific meaning when used in the world of mathematics, but that have another meaning when used in other *academic* fields or in conversation: *function, line, point, evaluate, improper,* etc.

- *Phrases of mathematics:* Words that, when put together, mean more than the sum of their parts; phrases are to be understood as a whole, as if they were single words: *common denominator, sum of the squares, lowest common multiple, linear equation,* etc.

Teaching the Words of Mathematics and the Academic Words Surrounding Them

How do words—any words—get learned and stay learned? And, what is specific about the words of mathematics—math words, we'll call them—that might deserve special consideration?

To shed light on how words get learned and stay learned, I will refer to the theories of Stephen Krashen (2004), whose work in the field of second language acquisition can be applied to learning technical terminology in one's native language. In other words, let's think about what works well in expanding language capacity in general, and then apply those principles to expanding our students' language capacity to include the language of the world of mathematics.

Krashen sets forth five hypotheses about second language acquisition. Let's look at each and consider its applicability to learning the words of mathematics.

Acquisition-Learning Hypothesis

This theory posits that we learn a second language in two ways. The first is naturally, by being exposed to the target language in a meaningful context. In the process of attempting to communicate in the target language, a person picks up both the words and the grammar of that language. The learner is concentrating on purpose-driven communication, not language acquisition, but language acquisition results naturally and unconsciously.

The second means of learning a language is through direct, orderly instruction in the target language.

As this applies to mathematics class, we already know what the direct, orderly instruction looks like. And we already rely heavily on this means: Picture the teacher—supplemented by her mathematics textbook—defining and giving examples and illustrations of the mathematical terms. This type of instruction could be made better by incorporating the etymologies of the mathematical terms so that they may be linked to other words already in the students' vocabulary. (See Appendix 1, page 101, for an annotated list of common word components used in mathematical language.) The more connections and associations that are made to *any* new terminology, the more memorable and meaningful the learning of the terms will be.

For teachers to improve their direct instruction in the vocabulary of mathematics, they need to learn more about how words of mathematics are connected to familiar words and expand their explanations accordingly. In so doing, they are building the habit in their students of making similar kinds of connections.

Now let's expand the model to incorporate natural language acquisition. When students are given opportunities to communicate in authentic problem-solving situations about mathematics, when they are listening to their teachers not as strictly information givers but as cosolvers of the problem, when students strive to express themselves mathematically, cued by a person fluent in the language of mathematics, we have what Krashen refers to as *acquisition*.

To illustrate, picture yourself in a cooking class. The master chef explains the key terms to be used in a recipe that you are about to prepare. These terms include terms about process (verbs): *stir*, *mix*, *separate*, *blend*, *blanche*. The terms refer to the ingredients and tools (nouns): *cilantro, shallots, Chinese eggplant, wok*. If you were not fluent in the language of cooking, you would learn the verbs by watching and doing the processes, and you would learn the nouns by seeing them. And, in the context of authentic communication, you would hear key words repeatedly. But you would hear not only these key words: you would hear a set of supportive words that are often used in the cooking field: words of sequence, words about temperature, words about the condition and texture of food. You would absorb more words than you realized. Some of these words would come into your full control; others, you would learn to a lesser degree, and you may come into full control of them as you continue your experiences and communication about cooking. By communication, we mean more than just listening to the master chef. To learn a language, we need to use the language as novices. A language learner needs to repeat directions, ask questions, create analogies, ask for clarification, rephrase information.

As it is with any specialized vocabulary, so it is with mathematical words! The more your students are given opportunities to engage in authentic communication in mathematics, the more their mathematical vocabulary will grow in depth and scope.

Monitor Hypothesis

Krashen's second theory is called the *monitor hypothesis*: This facet of language learning may be described as the development of intuition about what sounds right/what sounds wrong in the language and how to correct it. To develop the internal monitor that allows us to edit and correct our own language, we need to be steeped in the language. As students hear and read the language of mathematics, they develop their internal monitors only if they are given ample opportunities to use all four language capacities: listening and reading (receptive capacity), speaking and writing (productive capacity).

The interplay of all four language capacities is extremely important if we want students to become proficient in mathematics. The "old model" of teaching math relies on listening as the main language capacity. Reading may be done as part of homework, word problems, or using the textbook as a reference. Speaking is actually done very little, with a few students voicing questions and answers. Cooperative learning, which involves speaking among peers, is often regarded as "taking too long," "being disorganized," or "being disorderly." Writing is done rarely, except in geometric proofs or the labeling of steps when students are required to "show their work."

We can surmise that the sheer lack of experience in the four language capacities has a lot to do with the lack of development of the self-monitoring abilities that result from constant practice in the target language. To fix that, we need to weave listening, reading, speaking, and writing into mathematics classes, even if it "takes too much time." The time that it takes is a wise investment. In short, if students in mathematics class are too quiet, they may be too quiet to learn.

Natural Order Hypothesis

Krashen's third theory, the *natural order hypothesis*, has to do with the order in which speakers of a second language are likely to become grammatically proficient. Mathematical language has its own patterns, and those patterns form a kind of grammar. Although "math grammar" follows the patterns of English grammar (math grammar is not a *separate* kind of grammar) it does have its own preferred sentence structures, as follows:

- *Commands:* Many mathematical sentences begin with a verb that tells you what to do. In addition to the four operations—add, subtract, multiply, divide—we also encounter such commands as *find, evaluate, compare, solve, round, estimate, regroup, explain, undo, write, simplify, replace, reduce,* and *check.*

- *Definitions:* Definitions are not always presented as sentences. A definition begins with a noun or a noun phrase that is then placed in a genus (general category, such as *shape, process, condition*) and then refined into a species (*having three sides, of adding like numbers, in which all angles are congruent, etc.*).

- *Word problems:* Word problems usually begin with a simple statement that expresses some kind of condition: *Kyle has a half a tank of gas in his car.* This sentence is followed by details about the condition, expressed as a simple sentence, grammatically. The third sentence is likely to pose the problem in the form of a question. So, in a typical word problem, the student has to process the first two sentences to derive the information necessary to answer the question.

- *Syllogisms:* The famous *if...then* statement, known as a syllogism, is ever present in mathematics text.

Generally, sentences of mathematics have a simple grammatical structure that can be characterized as having short sentences and a clipped style. The syntax (sentence structure) of the mathematical language that we would find in a textbook is, in of itself, not unfamiliar or inaccessible to most native speakers. The syntax that they encounter in their English Language Arts classes—stories, dialogue, poetry—is far more complex. Strategy 3 will go further into mathematical syntax and its implications for reading comprehension.

Input Theory

Krashen's fourth theory, the *input* theory, posits that the learner will advance in the target language if given sufficient "comprehensible input" so that the learner can *use what the learner knows* to go to the next level. What this means in mathematics class is that enough of the mathematical language has to be nestled in familiar language so that the learner is challenged without being totally lost in new language. Comprehensible input can manifest as short, grammatically simple sentences; familiar vocabulary; easily accessible metaphors; internal "translations" or "in other words" statements. With enough of these, targeted mathematical terms may be understood. Everyone whose job it is to initiate the novice into the professional conversation needs to keep the input theory in mind as they speak.

Affective Filter Theory

Finally, Krashen's theory of the *affective filter* educates us about the deleterious effect that negative emotions have on learning. Negative emotions such as fear, nervousness, anger, resentment, feelings of inferiority, and a defeatist attitude impede the learner's ability to accept and remember new information. The wise and skillful mathematics teacher is keenly aware of how anxiety over the ability to learn and perform mathematically creates a mental block. She does everything possible to reduce math anxiety: reexplains; creates a positive and nonthreatening classroom climate; differentiates instruction; celebrates small moments of success; acknowledges progress; connects the new to the known.

You can see how all of these five theories of second language acquisition overlap and interlock. In summary, we can say that new language/new terminology of mathematics is greatly helped by:

- Integrating the four language capacities: listening and reading (receptive capacities) and speaking and writing (productive capacities).

- Connecting new language to known language.

- Using simple, predictable grammatical structures.

- Providing comprehensible input so that new language is nestled in enough familiar language to make the new language accessible.

Three Categories of Mathematical Words

Category 1: Words that We Encounter Almost Exclusively in Mathematics

We'll use the following body of words as our examples as we discuss the challenges and possibilities for students as they seek to bring these words meaningfully into their math vocabulary. These words are arranged alphabetically for convenience:

abacus	coplanar	histogram	pi
addend	cuboid	integer	pictograph
algorithm	decagon,	interval	polygon,
algebra	decahedron,	kilogram, kiloliter,	polyhedron
annulus	dodecahedron,	kilometer	quadrant,
axis	tetrahedron,	median	quadruple
bilateral,	hexahedron,	milligram,	quotient
unilateral,	icosahedron	milliliter,	radian, radius
quadrilateral,	decimal	millimeter	ratio
equilateral	declination	multilateral	rhombus
binary	denominator	multiplicand	seriate
binomial,	dividend	numerator	subset
polynomial	divisor	oblique	subtrahend
bisect/bisector	ellipse	oblong	tangram
circumference	equation	pantograph	tessellation
coefficient	exponent	parallelepiped,	transversal
collinear	factorization	parallelogram	trapezium,
concave	frustum	pentagon	trapezoid
convex	hectare	permutation	vertex
congruent,	heptagon	perpendicular	
congruency	hexagon,		
	hexagram		

Because we encounter these words almost exclusively in the world of mathematics, they are brand new. The student has not even heard them before. Let's consider the instructional implications for words that are being heard for the first time.

In the world of conversation and in the world of academic discourse, when we hear a word for the first time, it is usually used in context. Its context may or may not give good clues as to its meaning. Its meaning will emerge more clearly as we encounter the new word again and again. Because of multiple exposure and rich context, the newness of the word will wear off, and, seamlessly, it will become a known word, a word whose definition we have figured out unconsciously.

Not so with Category I mathematical words. For these words, a student's very first encounter may be an explicit definition. When we hear a word whose sound is new to us, we need exposures to that new sound, that new combination of morphemes and syllables. Without that repetition of sound, the unfamiliar word will fly right out of our heads.

Discovering a New Concept that Is Called by a New Word

To understand how best to teach a Category I mathematical word, and to have it stay learned, that is, discovering a new concept that is called by a new word, we should ask ourselves this question about the target word: Does this word name a new concept, refine a familiar concept, or simply name (or rename) an *already-known* concept?

These distinctions are important because we need to connect the new to the known. If the target word is new both in sound and in meaning, then we need to find some way to link the concept to known information.

In addition, let's consider the degree of familiarity in the morphology of the word. A word like *algebra* is new in sound; none of its word components link to any other word components in meaning. A word like *trigonometry*, however, may be new in its combination of sounds, but its components may be linked to known information: *tri-* for *three*; *-gon* for *form*; *metr-* for *measurement*. Therefore, when the student finds out that trigonometry has to do with triangles and something to do with measurements, she can link new to known in a way that cannot be done to the more opaque word, *algebra*. Although a student might guess that the word algebra has something to do with *algae* and something to do with a *bra*, that guess would happen to be wrong, albeit the thinking behind such a guess would be laudable, if not to say highly amusing. We teach students to be word detectives—to look for and listen to sound-alikes inside the word and to attempt connections. That is not to say that the connections will always be valid. (Incidentally, the word *algebra* hails from the Arabic language, which has far fewer English cognates than the ancestors of the Greco-Roman *trigonometry*.) The following box points out the importance of including etymology in our discussion of mathematical language.

> **What Does Etymology Have to Do with Mathematics?**
>
> There are those who dismiss etymology of mathematical words as a "nice-to-know" option, a luxury that the "cover-the-curriculum" clock does not permit. However, teaching a bit about the derivation of *any* word offers insights that increase the likelihood that the word will be remembered and understood on a deeper level. A word is more than a bunch of sounds: Words, especially technical ones, are artifacts whose histories reveal inner truths and subtleties. Just as we learn more about people when we meet their families, we learn more about words when we understand how their roots and components are connected to words having a similar background. Appendix 1, page 101, offers a handful of word histories for mathematical language. Consider it a starter kit as you build and share your knowledge about the etymology of mathematical words with your students.

Refining a Known Concept with a New Word

The word *parallelogram* refines a familiar concept. The familiar concept is that of a four-sided figure. But a parallelogram is not just *any* four-sided figure, nor is there only one kind of parallelogram. Here, the student possesses the concept of the four-sided figure and narrows four-sided figures down only to those that meet the criteria for a parallelogram. This kind of word is a good example of the importance of visualization when it comes to many mathematical terms. The language that defines a parallelogram—although it can, like any bit of language, be memorized—is likely to be meaningless without multiple diagrams that can be "snapshotted" in the brain and retrieved whenever the conversation comes round to parallelograms (as math conversations are wont to do).

Naming a Known Concept with a New Word

The word *rhombus* encapsulates an existing concept, one that is known, but heretofore unnamed. Being unnamed, it is more than likely to lie outside one's conscious thoughts. Being unnamed, it has no mental boundary, no mental drawer, so to speak. It's unlikely that the average person is going to think about forms in the shape of a rhombus without having the word rhombus to name that shape. And thus it is with the power of language: Language allows us to access thoughts, even before we communicate them.

And there's a thrill in finding out that something that we kind of "knew," but never really thought about, in fact, has a name. It's as though a reality that we had inside of us is not our own unique experience, but something that others experience in a similar way. *"Oh, that has a name!"*

Now let's think about what's going on internally within our mathematics vocabulary. I mentioned earlier that just because the parts of a word sound like parts of another word, it does not mean that a meaning-based connection is there; however, we need to instill in our students the habit of looking for those connections. That habit would, of course, be predicated on their knowing the common word components of mathematics. It goes without saying that students should be thoroughly familiar with the Greco-Latinate prefixes that represent numbers: *uni-*, *bi-*, *di-*, *tri-*, *quadr-*, etc. In Appendix 1 (page 101), I lay out numerous other mathematics-related word components, along with what I'm calling "surprising connections." These connections may or may not be surprising to you: you may already be in the habit of connecting words in your head by understanding how words are related through component parts. I'm assuming that your students may not have cultivated this mentally productive habit, and they will indeed find the connections surprising and illuminating. In any case, the connectedness is what will make their word knowledge deeper and more durable. Appendix 1 details common word components used in mathematics and suggests connections.

Category 2: Words with Multiple Meanings Outside of the World of Mathematics

Students come to you knowing how to use the word property in the sentence "Get off my property." They may know what it means to "express their feelings" or "have a surprised expression." They may know what the "value of a gift" is. But they may not know how words like *property*, *expression*, and *value* narrow their meanings to apply only to mathematics.

area	gross	property
average	like	range
base	mean	rational
content	mode	real
degree	negative	root
evaluate	operation	set
expression	origin	term
factor	positive	value
figure	power	volume
function	product	

It would be impossible to list all of the mathematics terms that have a broader meaning outside of mathematics, but a list like this gives us another way of looking at and teaching mathematics terms deeply, rather than superficially. When a word is used in more than one context, there is usually a link between the word's general and specific meanings. While it is true that we want students to learn and apply the mathematic-specific meaning to a word, it would be more than foolish to deny that the general meaning connects to the mathematical meaning. They key is to find that link. Doing so will yield a deeper understanding of how the word is used in a mathematics context.

We should not let students think that their outside knowledge is irrelevant to mathematics, that they should leave their experience and intuition in their lockers when they come to mathematics class. When we help students understand that a word can have both a broad meaning and a narrow meaning, we help them become flexible, adaptable thinkers. The graphic organizer shown in Figure 1.1 can help students link prior knowledge to domain-specific knowledge of mathematical words.

Figure 1.1. Words with Multiple Meanings

Math Meaning	Conversational Meaning
Visual	Visual

Math Sentence:
_____
_____
_____

Conversational Sentence:
_____
_____
_____

Category 3: Phrases of Mathematics

You are familiar with the concept of sight words. Sight words are words that appear *frequently* in written text, but that cannot be learned through phonics. Students learn the sight words by repeated exposure (drill and practice). You are probably also familiar with the concept of chunking text, which means that the reader processes several words at a glance, rather than be reading word by word. Well, in mathematical language, we have a plethora of terms that consist of phrases. These phrases have to be processed as a unit, not as single words. These phrases mean something other than the sum of their individual words. We will call them flash phrases because the reader has to recognize and process them in a *flash* rather than word by word.

The following are examples of flash phrases of mathematics:

absolute value	coordinate plane	scientific notation
square root	cube root	number squared
adjacent angles	complementary	acute angle
supplementary angles	angles	congruent angles
isosceles triangle	obtuse angle	equilateral triangle
composite numbers	parallel lines	perpendicular lines
natural numbers	irrational numbers	mixed number
whole numbers	prime numbers	real numbers
irrational numbers	proper fraction	improper fraction
more than, less than	least common denominator	greatest common multiple

Flash cards, word games, classroom posters, and other visuals and meaningful repetition help students think of these phrases as single words to make them immediately recognizable.

Numbers and Counting

Lucky are the children who come to school counting. From their earliest days, they may have had parents and others who tended to them who led them into the world of counting through nursery rhymes and play. The cadence of the number system—the feel of counting—is ingrained in them long before their first day of kindergarten. Chances are that children's ability to attain a school-ready understanding of numbers, counting, measurement, and quantification also have a sense of story text. They know what the language of a story sound like because they have been generously read to since babyhood.

One of the greatest challenges educators face is bringing children up to speed when they come to school without the rhythms of language and numbers (and the language *of* numbers). A smart way to meet two needs with one activity is by immersing children in stories that embed numbers. In their book, *New Visions for Linking Literature and Mathematics* (2004), David J. and Phillis Whitin offer a lengthy annotated bibliography of children's books that weave the language and concepts of numbers into their stories.

What is the vocabulary of numbers? First, we learn to name the numbers and see the patterns. While it's easy to see how the *twenties, thirties, forties,* etc., correspond to two, *three, four*, etc., it may not occur to many children (or adults, for that matter) that the *teens* are connected linguistically to the word *ten*! Or that the word *twelve* is related to the word *two*! I'll admit that the *teen–ten* connection never occurred to me until I began thinking about number systems in the process of writing this book! Although I consider myself knowledgeable about the English language and its etymology, no one had ever pointed this connection out to me, and so I never thought of it myself. Knowing it now makes the number system seem even more systematic.

So what is the vocabulary of the number system? We speak of real numbers as being divided into natural and irrational numbers, but this is circular to the child hearing it for the first time. What numbers wouldn't be real? If a number itself is not real, what is it? The words *rational* and *irrational* are highly abstract. In the nonmathematical world, they have to do with sanity and insanity, but those associations do not help us understand rationality in the mathematical world. It's tempting to dismiss the relationship between a *rational* person and a *rational* number. But the dictionary reveals a common ancestry that illuminates, rather than separates, the meaning of both—the great, great granddaddy of the word *rational* is its root that means *judge, estimate, reason*. The moral of the story is that words that are long and strange have ancestral clues to their meaning. (Appendix 1, page 101, explores the etymology of mathematical words extensively.)

I recently met an excellent mathematics teacher in an urban setting who told me how he explains the word *geometry* to his students. He writes the word on the board (visual cue) and asks the students to tell him what they know. Most respond that they know that geometry was all about shapes. Then he asks if they knew what the *geo* part means. They do know that geo means *earth*, as in *geology*. "Well," he says, "when you look outside, do you see a bunch of shapes?" The students note that the shapes that they see outside are mostly manmade ones, buildings and such. The mathematics teacher then leads them into a little history lesson about how the concept of geometry originated in the Nile River Valley at the dawn of civilization, when farms—and therefore land ownership—sprang up by the river, for the obvious reason of irrigation. But when the Nile flooded its banks, there went the lines of division from one farm to the next. Hence, a system was needed to measure (*-metry*) the land (*geo*). There you have it!

Again, the purpose of using etymology to teach vocabulary is that stories are memorable and connectedness helps the world make sense. Academic language is full of Latin and Greek word components which, if known, put the learner at a tremendous advantage when it comes to learning polysyllabic words. Thus, the unabridged dictionary, as well as a good dictionary of Greek and Latin word roots, are the mathematics teacher's friends.

Here's a maxim: Never teach just one word! What I mean is never teach a single word all by itself, as if it had no relatives. All polysyllabic words, and many monosyllabic ones as well, have roots and tendrils connecting them to other words.

Conclusion

I'm hoping that, after reading this chapter, you will view yourself as a lifelong learner of words, specifically the words relevant to mathematics. I'm hoping that you pursue etymology as an endlessly interesting source that illuminates the meaning of words, especially polysyllabic ones. And I'm hoping that you will slow down to teach words explicitly, with the faith that time spent illuminating meanings of mathematical words will pay back as your students learn to "speak math fluently."

STRATEGY 2

Teaching Academic Words Implicitly

Excellent teachers of mathematics use plain English to teach academic words implicitly. There are two categories of vocabulary instruction: *explicit* and *implicit*. This chapter addresses implicit vocabulary instruction, which means learning words through natural exposure and opportunities for use over time. If we were talking about learning a foreign language, implicit word learning would go by the term *immersion*.

In a way, we *are* talking about learning a foreign language—the language of academic English. The mathematical terms that we addressed in Strategy 1 do not appear in isolation. Consider the wording of a problem like this:

> Using information from the table, write an equation that represents the balance, b, in Jeffrey's bank account as a function of the number of weeks, w.

Hopefully, the student has been taught the mathematically relevant meaning of the words *table, equation, balance,* and *function*. But does he know what *represent* means in this context? His teachers may assume that, somewhere along the line, he has either been taught *represent* in a mathematical context, or he has been able to figure it out. Is that assumption correct?

I'm sure you've had the experience of administering a test and having to answer questions from nervous, naïve, and baffled students like: What does *represent* mean? What does *identify* mean? What does *adequate* mean? What does *determine* mean? What does *indicate* mean? Granted, in a testing situation, students get stressed and doubt their intuition about words that they actually do know. And granted, students often don't recognize a word in print when they do know it when they hear it. But academic discourse is characterized by a set of words that supports the work we do to teach the mathematical terms. Mathematical terms appear in the context of an elevated academic language register. But are we supposed to teach them all of these academic words as well as the mathematical terms!? After reading Strategy 1, you may already despair of ever having enough time to teach the mathematical terms, let alone the academic words that surround them.

Let's do some math here. A study done at the University of Oregon references the work of Hart and Risley (1995) on the "meaningful differences" in vocabulary between children at the time they enter school. Let's look at the language experiences of three hypothetical children: Alison, Bradley, and Cecilia.

If Alison is a child whose household depends on public assistance, Hart and Risley's statistics show that she hears about 616 words per day from her parents or caretakers. Bradley, whose household can be said to be "working class," hears 1,251 words. And Cecilia, whose household can be said to be "professional," hears 2,153 words.

When Alison is 3 years old, she will know 600 fewer words than Cecilia does, and by the time both girls are in second grade, Alison will trail Cecilia by 2,000 words. That gap will continue to grow, with Alison's reading development lagging and Cecilia's reading comprehension flourishing accordingly. Cecilia will enter kindergarten with about 6,000 words under her belt; Alison, with as few as 3,000; Bradley somewhere in between.

It is estimated that, to do well academically, children need to pick up about eight words per day (3,000 per year). If you calculate that out, you'll see that we're talking about nonschool days as well. The more they fall behind in that accumulation, the more deficient their reading (also known as *information processing*) skills will become. The result of the vocabulary gap is that those with poor vocabularies tend to like reading less, tend to read less, and thus fall further and further behind their peers who do like to read, read, and pick up more and more words and background knowledge on the variety of subjects that they read about.

Add that to the fact that Cecilia will go home every day to the same language-rich family that delivered her to school with a hearty vocabulary to begin with, and that Cecilia's education-minded and well-to-do parents and grandparents fill the bookshelves in her room with volumes of literature.

What Can Be Done to Bridge the Vocabulary Gap?

It is extremely important that every teacher understand how the vocabulary gap, related to economic circumstances for whatever reason, affects students' achievement in school. It is extremely important that every teacher do all that is possible to expose children to vocabulary that is as rich as possible. As a person teaching mathematics, your role in teaching general academic words is supportive, not primary. By consciously elevating your language tone and at the same time using language that is comprehensible to the students, you can make a big difference in their ability to handle the academic language that surrounds your mathematical terms.

We have an incredibly valuable and no-cost resource to enrich academic vocabulary. The Academic Word List (Coxhead, 2000), commonly called the AWL, is a well-organized list of the 570 words that are *not* within the 2,000 most frequently used words in English conversational speech, but that *are* frequently used in academic discourse, based on college text books. Students who are fluent on the AWL are much more likely to be successful in all academic areas than those who are not thoroughly familiar and conversant on these words. The words are drawn from all areas of academic discourse, not just mathematics.

As presented below, the AWL is organized into ten subsets, according to the frequency of the words in academic text. Within each subset, the words are organized alphabetically. To summarize: Ordinary conversation in English takes in approximately 2,000 to 3,000 words. That set of conversational words is known as BICS (Basic Interpersonal Communication Set). Academic discourse encompasses an additional set of words, known as CALPS (Cognitive Academic Language Proficiency Set). The AWL (Academic Word List) is a scientifically deduced list of the 570 most commonly used words in CALPS. The AWL is arranged in order of frequency of word use in academic discourse, with Subset 1 as those words that are used most frequently, through Subset 10 as those words that are used least frequently of these 570 most frequently used words in academic discourse.

The Academic Word List (AWL)

- *Subset 1*—analyze, approach, area, assess, assume, available, benefit, concept, consist, context, constitute, contract, data, define, derive, distribute, economy, establish, estimate, evident, factor, finance, formula, function, income, indicate, individual, interpret, involve, issue, principle, proceed, process, require, research, respond, section, sector, significant, similar, source, specific, structure, vary

- *Subset 2*—acquire, affect, appropriate, aspect, assist, category, chapter, commission, complex, compute, conclude, conduct, consequent, construct, consume, credit, design, distinct, equate, element, evaluate, final, invest, item, maintain, normal, obtain, perceive, positive, potential, previous, primary, purchase, range, region, regulate, relevant, restrict, seek, select, strategy, survey, transfer

- *Subset 3*—alternative, circumstance, compensate, component, considerable, constant, contribute, coordinate, criteria, deduce, demonstrate, dominate, emphasis, justify, layer, link, maximize, minor, negate, outcome, proportion, react, secure, shift, specify, sufficient, task, technique, technology, valid, volume

- *Subset 4*—access, adequacy, annual, apparent, approximate, attribute, code, commit, communicate, concentrate, confer, contrast, cycle, despite, dimension, emerge, error, goal, grant, hence, hypothesis, implement, implicate, impose, integrate, internal, investigate, job, label, mechanism, obvious, parallel, parameter, phase, predict, prior, principal, project, promote, resolve, retain, series, statistic, status, stress, subsequent, sum, summary, undertake

- *Subset 5*—adjust, alter, amend, capacity, challenge, compound, conflict, contact, decline, discrete, enable, energy, equivalent, fundamental, generate, generation, image, logic, margin, mental, modify, monitor, network, notion, objective, orient, perspective, precise, prime, pursue, ratio, reject, revenue, stable, substitute, sustain, symbol, target, transit, trend, version, whereas

- *Subset 6*—abstract, accuracy, aggregate, allocate, assign, attach, bond, brief, cooperate, discriminate, display, diverse, domain, edit, exceed, explicit, flexible, furthermore, interval, migrate, minimum, neutral, precede, rational , reveal, scope, subsidy, trace, transform

- *Subset 7*—comprehensive, comprise, confirm, contrary, convert, decade, definite, differentiate, dispose, dynamic, eliminate, extract, finite, foundation, grade, identical, insert, isolate, mode, paradigm

- *Subset 8*—accumulate, chart, commodity, complement, currency, detect, deviate, displace, eventual, fluctuate, manipulate, minimize, radical, random, schedule, terminate, uniform, via, visual, widespread

- *Subset 9*—analogy, coincide, compatible, concurrent, converse, protocol, supplement, temporary, sphere, unify, portion, preliminary, mediate, medium, format, overlap, revolution, integral, intermediate, subordinate, duration, diminish

- *Subset 10*—adjacent, assemble, collapse, compile, depress, incline, whereas

As we look over the list, we find many words that we would teach explicitly in a mathematical context. In Subset 5 alone, we find *equivalent, expand, orient, perspective, prime, ratio,* and *revenue.* Although these might qualify as true "math words," the linguistic research in academic discourse concludes that they are used extensively in other subject areas as well. On the AWL, we find words that are necessary for understanding how the mathematical words might be used in context. Such words, again from Subset 5 alone, include *adjust, amend, aware, capacity, compound,* and *conflict,* to name a handful.

Because this is a book about teaching mathematics, I've shortened the AWL, eliminating some words that don't usually apply to mathematics. You may be interested to know the other words in the AWL:

legislate	administrate	tradition	authority	devote
environment	labor	legal	policy	qualitative
role	theory	achieve	aspect	insight
community	culture	feature	focus	manual
impact	institute	injure	journal	conceive
participate	reside	resource	secure	intrinsic
site	text	constrain	convene	likewise
core	corporate	document	partner	confine
philosophy	publish	scheme	technical	violate
comment	consent	physical	register	refine
rely	attitude	civil	debate	distort
domestic	ethnic	regime	professional	mature
academy	aware	clause	draft	convince
enforce	entity	evolve	image	integrity
liberal	license	medical	monitor	nonetheless
psychology	style	welfare	acknowledge	controversy
overseas	nevertheless	presume	recover	trigger
federal	scope	enhance	ignorance	restrain
cite	estate	gender	lecture	erode
minister	motive	transport	utilize	albeit
underlie	adapt	adult	advocate	encounter
aid	channel	chemical	classic	invoke
empirical	equip	file	guarantee	notwithstanding
hierarchy	ideology	infer	innovate	device
intervene	media	phenomenon	publication	vision
release	thesis	topic	priority	inherent
prohibit	simulate	submit	successor	scenario
transmit	ultimate	unique	abandon	colleague
accompany	ambiguous	appreciate	appendix	forthcoming
arbitrary	automate	bias	clarify	levy
conform	contemporary	contradict	denote	ongoing
exhibit	exploit	guideline	highlight	panel
implicit	induce	inevitable	infrastructure	so-called
inspect	intense	nuclear	offset	persist
paragraph	practitioner	predominant	prospect	straightforward
reinforce	restore	revise	tense	pose
theme	thereby	accommodate	anticipate	whereby
assure	attain	behalf	cease	reluctance
			commence	

Let's return to Stephen Krashen's principle of natural language acquisition through comprehensible input. In a language-rich mathematics class, you would see the comprehensible input principle enacted as *repeated, meaningful, context-rich exposure to AWL words:* If a speaker's vocabulary runs "a little beyond" the existing vocabulary of the listener, the listener's vocabulary will improve. An ordinary person (not a teacher) employs his or her vocabulary without conscious regard for how much new vocabulary is being heard by the listener. But a skillful teacher develops habits of communication that recruits and supports vocabulary that the listener doesn't know, or doesn't know fully, but needs to know.

A person's existing vocabulary acts as a wick to absorb new vocabulary that burns around it until becoming part of the flame. While novice or unskilled teachers consciously *lower* the level of vocabulary that they use in their speech and writing to students, skillful teachers wisely and skillfully *elevate* theirs, supplying enough context to clarify meanings.

Armed with the AWL, teachers can give students concentrated doses of the language necessary for their success. She might post the words, subset by subset, in the classroom and on her website. She might make it her business to include a smattering of the words, subset by subset, in her speech every day. If the words are used repeatedly in a natural manner, subset by subset, students will absorb them unconsciously. The value of making it a practice to focus on one subset at a time—say for one week each—is that doing so provides that concentrated does that ensures meaningful repetition.

In the ideal school, all teachers would be aware of the AWL. All teachers would incorporate the words naturally. They would enter into the kind of conspiracy where students would be hearing and seeing the level of language represented by the AWL. In schools where students are especially low-performing, for whatever reason, the culprit is often the lack of an academic vocabulary. If teachers throughout the district were to focus on one subset each week and then repeat the cycle, students would receive concentrated doses of the academic language they so desperately need in a manner that is efficient, painless, and even inexpensive. I can't think of another intervention so easy to administer and so powerful.

Conclusion

I hope that as a result of reading this chapter you have a better idea of how you can improve your students' ability to comprehend mathematics by enriching the language that they hear in your class. By developing the "teacherly habit" of upgrading your speech to include the words on the Academic Word List while supporting those words with familiar language, you can help to bridge that all-important vocabulary gap that researchers have brought to our attention. The vocabulary gap is the major factor affecting poor reading comprehension, and poor reading comprehension is a major culprit in overall poor achievement in school. We cannot teach explicitly all the words that students need to know. But we can immerse our students in the kind of academic words that they need to access content in mathematics and every other subject.

STRATEGY 3

Reinforcing Reading Comprehension Skills that Apply to Mathematics

Excellent teachers of mathematics use plain English to reinforce reading comprehension skills that apply to math-related text. Excellent teachers prepare the student for the reading task—to enter, as it were, the *mental reading room*. By that, I'm referring to the mindset that allows new information to be piped in from an outside source (the author).

Reading text in mathematics is not like reading literary text. It is much slower and more recursive. Reading comprehension is shaped by the reader's purpose. Our purpose for reading directs our focus and determines what we take from the reading experience. We read the mathematics textbook to solve a problem directly, or to prepare ourselves to be able to solve a problem eventually. Where there's mathematics, there are problems to solve, and that is why the texts of mathematics, unlike literary text, exist. (Literary text exists to engage the reader in an imaginary world.) So, the math reader's guiding question must be: How will this information help me solve problems? or, in the case of actual word problems: *What is the problem to be solved? What information is relevant to solving the problem? What am I supposed to do with this information?*

What We Mean by "Teaching Reading in the Content Areas"

No one expects teachers of mathematics to become true reading teachers. But to the extent that reading the mathematics textbook is a specialized skill, excellent mathematics teachers include reading-in-math instruction as an integral problem-solving skill.

Ideas about what it actually means to "teach reading" have changed. There are those who still think that "teaching reading" means only teaching decoding, which would involve such things as phonics and drilling sight words. By the time students reach the upper elementary grades, such reading instruction is necessary only for those students who are significantly below grade level.

Today, when we talk about "teaching reading in the content areas," in this case, in mathematics, we are talking about helping students create the lifelong mental habits that will result in comprehension and retention. It really should be called "information processing," but because the information that we're talking about is delivered through reading, we do call it "reading comprehension."

The outdated concept of reading comprehension instruction may have consisted of students reading isolated texts (referred to as "passages") about random topics and then answering multiple choice questions that fell into certain categories: discerning the main idea, understanding the role of supportive detail, figuring out how a word is used in context, distinguishing between fact and opinion, making inferences based on reasonable assumptions, and perceiving the author's tone and purpose. Although these kinds of questions are still asked in reading comprehension standardized tests, and although deriving this kind of information is the essence of understanding text, we now come at instruction through a different paradigm.

Today, the words "reading comprehension instruction" and "embedding reading instruction in the content areas" should evoke a set of mental processes (strategies) that skilled readers use to extract meaning from text. In my book, *But I'm Not a Reading Teacher* (Larchmont, NY: Eye On Education), I explain these reading strategies in terms of where they fall in the reading process: before, during, and after reading. In my workshops, I recommend thinking of the reading process as consisting of three Cs:

- Before Reading: Connect!
- During Reading: Concentrate!
- After Reading: Communicate!

Before Reading: Connect!

Connection 1: Background Knowledge and Key Vocabulary

By now, everyone knows the value of background knowledge as it applies to information processing: The more we know about a given subject, the more easily we can learn and retain more information about it. Conversely, a critical gap between the knowledge that the author/speaker expects the reader/listener to have can prevent comprehension. It is the lack of background knowledge that leads us to frown in frustration and say things like

"What are you even talking about?" and "I didn't understand one word of that!"

We need to give students enough of a boost to give them a toehold into whatever it is that they are about to read. In other words, we need to tell them in advance, to a certain extent, what the text is about. It may seem like we are doing too much of the work for them—spoon-feeding them, as some say. If that is your concern, think about your own reading habits. When you read editorials in the newspaper, do you ever read about things that you know nothing about? Unlikely. You probably read about subjects that are already familiar enough to you that you are merely adding to a storehouse of knowledge and informed opinions. Try reading an editorial about a subject that is as unfamiliar to you as possible and think about how you would fare on a typical comprehension test, as compared to how you would do on a comprehension test about a subject to which you brought substantial background knowledge. Providing students with background knowledge before their reading experiences makes the information accessible.

But how best to provide background knowledge prior to a reading experience? And how to do it in a way that will not devour our allocated math time? By the time students reach the upper elementary and middle school grades, they have been given many K-W-L charts.*

In my workshops, I use a few variations on the theme of the K-W-L chart, especially to elicit prior knowledge about my topic. If I were to give out the K-W-L chart in its familiar format, teachers might feel patronized. To put a twist on it, I place a sheet of chart paper and markers on the tables and ask teachers to create an Alpha Board (Figure 3.1, page 24), which takes just a few minutes. They use the Alpha Board to quickly jot down words and phrases representing what they know about the topic at hand. Then, we post these on the walls and simply give them a glance. This little community-building, low-tech exercise brings us into the field and exercises our creative-thinking muscles as a way of getting started. To use the Alpha Board, just jot down words about the day's topic that begin with the letters in each box. This is a brainstorming activity.

If you do a similar thing for mathematics before introducing a unit, you have established the first of the four connections that I am recommending as "before reading" strategies. One of its advantages is that it reduces math anxiety before a new unit because the Alpha Board strategy elicits what students *do* know. (They are about to feel bombarded with language and concepts they *don't* know.)

---

* A K-W-L chart is a graphic organizer with three columns. It is used to elicit what a student knows (K), wants to know (W), and has learned (L) about a topic. K-W-L charts are extremely popular and effective in elementary classrooms. Your students are probably familiar with them.

Figure 3.1. Alpha Board to Elicit Background Knowledge

Field: Triangles

AB angles acute angles	CD coordinating closed	EF equilateral
GH hypotenuse	IJK isosceles	LM line
NO obtuse angle	PQR Pythagorean theorem right	ST sides three scalene
UV vertical	WXYZ xyz angles	

I know well that the world of mathematics for the struggling student is a place where being wrong happens all too often. What the Alpha Board experience offers is a way to start off a unit feeling equipped with some knowledge and language. It's hard, if not impossible, to be "wrong" on the Alpha Board. And because it's cooperative learning, it's low risk.

Here are some other ways to bring forth background knowledge to connect to upcoming text:

- *Free association:* Just ask, "What words come to mind when I say…?" Free association allows for personal connections, visualization, review of recently learned and embedded concepts, even emotional responses that can impede or encourage future learning. Have fun with it. Have students call off words and phrases as they toss a beach ball. When the body loosens up, the mind does as well.

- *Metaphorical thinking:* The best way I know to evoke metaphorical thinking is to show a picture that represents the metaphor I have in mind. For example, in my presentations about teaching vocabulary, I show a picture of some gardening tools and ask my audience why they think I'm showing gardening tools at the beginning of a workshop about vocabulary instruction. What I was originally going for was the word *cultivation* (as in, we *cultivate* our students' vocabulary, we grow it with deliberate attention and informed techniques—we don't just throw a bunch of words at them and expect language growth to happen). But what I've found is better than that: What I've found is that I get all kind of interesting responses when I invite people to think metaphorically. People have said things like "We need different kinds of tools to teach vocabulary." "Vocabulary words have roots." "Gardening tools have specific names." "Vocabulary learning happens naturally." Metaphorical thinking invites the creative side of the mathematical mind to play.

- *Strangers/acquaintances/friends:* This strategy is the mirror image of free association. We give students a voluminous list of words and phrases relevant to the upcoming reading and ask them to designate each as a Stranger (never heard of it), Acquaintance (heard of it, don't know much about it), or Friend (know it). This strategy makes an excellent formative assessment. Have students revisit their Strangers/Acquaintances/Friends charts at various points in the unit to track their progress.

- *Anecdotes relevant to the topic:* Stories have a natural appeal. When you tell a story in mathematics class, students may expect that the story is going to lead to a problem for them to solve. But that doesn't have to be the case. Here, the story is a lead-in to what they are about to read. For example, Mrs. H is about to begin the chapter on Ratio and Proportion with her Algebra I class. She connects students to the text by telling about her grocery store experience. The store nearest to her house was offering a 25% discount on her favorite ice cream (Mouse Tracks). But a store three miles up the road was offering a pretty good knockoff, Monkey Bars, at "buy four, get one free." Factoring in the price of gasoline to travel to the farther-away store, this became an intriguing little mathematical problem that led into the targeted themes of ratio and proportion that students could certainly relate to.

Connection 2: Establish a Purpose for Reading

As mentioned earlier, the purpose that we set for reading shapes the meaning we get from the text. The purpose for reading Chapter 6 of the Integrated Algebra I text differs from the purpose for reading Chapter 6 of *The Scarlet Letter*. But struggling readers might not have the repertoire of reading skills to adjust their reading pace and focus to suit the purpose.

Obviously, you as the teacher need to know what your students' purpose would be for reading a chapter in the textbook, as opposed to their purpose for reading, say, a newspaper article about mathematics, or a word problem.

- You may want them to read the chapter of the textbook to overview what they will be learning. You might say: "Skim Chapter 6. Look at the pictures and the headings. When an artist paints a picture, she first makes a rough sketch. She intends to build details, one by one, over this sketch. Make a mental sketch of the chapter on the Pythagorean Theorem so you have something to build on when we talk about it in detail over the coming two weeks." Purpose for reading? Making a mental sketch: getting a very broad idea of the content.

- You may want students to read Chapter 6 after you've taught about the Pythagorean Theorem. Purpose for reading? Reinforcement through review: Determine what you understand about the Pythagorean Theorem and what you don't.

- You may want students to read Chapter 6 as a reference as they work through their homework. Purpose for reading? To find information immediately relevant to particular problems.

These are three very different reading purposes calling for different reading styles: reading for generalities, reading for reinforcement, reading for problem-solving. Other purposes for reading the mathematics textbook might be to:

- Figure out what problem I'm being asked to solve.
- Look for evidence relevant to this problem.
- Determine what I do understand and what I don't; formulate specific questions.
- Think about how I might explain this to someone else.

Connection 3: Think About the Genre (Establish Expectations)

Zigzag Reading

When you get behind the wheel of a car and make your way down highways and byways, your awareness of the kind of road you are on is essential to being a skilled driver: Are you driving along a country road? Expect curves and darting squirrels. In a suburban subdivision? Watch out for children. City streets? Expect the unexpected taxicab, pothole, and pedestrian. Interstate highway? Try not to get behind those eighteen-wheelers. Just as we don't drive in the same style on every kind of roadway, skilled readers build awareness of text types (genres) and adjust their pace and focus accordingly.

The mathematics textbook is unique. It's been said that we don't "read," we "work" it. The mathematics textbook almost always requires what I'll be calling "zigzag" reading.

Zigzag reading is the kind of reading that we do when we go back and forth from text to something else, such as a diagram or our own figurings. Zigzag reading, while being the main way most people read the mathematics textbook, is not the way we read stories. Students need to name, learn, and practice zigzag reading.

The genres within mathematics textbooks include directions/procedures, explanations (especially definitions), and word problems. Directions/procedures require zigzagging from text to your own progress as you work out the problem on paper. Explanations and definitions are usually accompanied by a diagram, and both text and diagram (zigzagging) are probably necessary to understanding. Word problems usually require several rereadings, as follows:

- *First reading:* Skim the problem to get your mind into its content. What is it about? Can you picture the situation?

- *Subsequent readings:* Determine what you are being asked to find out. Establish a ballpark figure about the answer. Is the answer to the problem likely to be more or less than the key number(s) in the problem?

- *Strategize:* What steps and operations will you use to solve the problem? Eliminate irrelevant information. Focus on relevant information.

As a teacher of mathematics, you are as accustomed to the genre as a New York City cab driver is to rush hour traffic. But your students may be as unprepared for its challenges as a newly licensed driver from the suburbs. It may seem a simple matter of "just follow the signs," but the novice may not even know where the signs are, not to mention that some signs may be obscured or missing.

So reading mathematics is something like city driving: It takes a surprisingly long time to cover just a little bit of territory, and you have to read your signs!

Connection 4: Overview

Yes, it's easier to comprehend something when you already know what it's about. Although everyone would agree with this statement (Thank you, Captain Obvious!), not every reader or every teacher takes full advantage of its truth.

Think about the role that "getting an overview" plays in other areas of our lives. When we go to a theatrical event (movie, concert, etc.), we have at least a general idea of what it will be about. When we travel, we usually glance over—if not actually pour over—information about what we are about to see and experience.

To get an overview of a chapter in a mathematics textbook, all we have to do is look at the main headings and subheadings. Ask your students to do this, taking only two minutes to do so. Then, ask them to tell you in a few words what the chapter is about. That's all there is to this step in the prereading process, but it can effect significant improvement in comprehension.

Although the above four connecting strategies may seem daunting or time-consuming, they are overlapping and mutually supportive, so you shouldn't need more than ten minutes at the most to connect your students to the text before having them read it.

During Reading: Concentrate!

During reading, the student is on her own. She needs to engage in mental behaviors that promote concentration and active meaning making. These behaviors begin with adjusting the environment to be conducive to reading: well-lit, free of distractions. And because reading in mathematics is different from reading for pleasure, there needs to be a math-friendly environment: a writing surface, sharp pencil, calculator, measuring tools, etc. Reading mathematics is not the cozy "reading corner" experience that reading a story is. The reader of mathematics needs space on which to write, measure, and figure.

A word about distractions. We've all seen students who swear that listening to music while doing homework helps them concentrate. Many adults believe this as well. While we can find studies on the effects of music on concentration, the results are inconclusive: What kind of music affects what kinds of people doing what kinds of tasks? Because I believe that the ability to concentrate when doing mental tasks—reading and doing mathematics—

I hesitate to "just say OK" when it comes to students being plugged in to headphones while they claim to be reading. Perhaps this is an opportunity for students to do some action research, comparing their comprehension and accuracy with and without listening to various kinds of music. The argument about the effects of music on concentration will continue, and earbuds will become increasingly invisible, but can we at least say no *dancing* while reading or doing math?

Visualizing and predicting are considered strategies that take place during reading. However, Stephen Krashen asserts that these behaviors are really natural practices that the active reader cannot help doing, and therefore are not strategies. The fact is: if you are not visualizing or anticipating (predicting), then you are not reading. The act of reading is the act of making meaning. Making meaning involves visualizing and anticipating, whenever language is involved. Therefore, visualizing and predicting can be thought of as metacognitive strategies, the mental habit of asking yourself, "Am I understanding?" The answer to that question is found in the answers to the questions "Am I visualizing what I'm reading?" and "Am I anticipating what's coming next?"

The reader who is drawing blanks on these questions needs to self-remediate: reread, adjust the environment, take notes, take a break.

After Reading: Communicate!

If we want students to retain what they've read, they need to solidify their understanding by explaining what they've read. Their explanation can be verbal or in writing. What they need to communicate is the main idea of what they've read, and here are two efficient structures for doing so:

- Outlining
- Paraphrasing: reword and regroup

Outlining to Communicate Understanding of Text

I'm a great believer in the power of outlining as a study skill to reinforce understanding of text. In fact, the act of creating an outline is, in itself, a powerful means of forcing oneself to think about main ideas and supportive details. And isn't outlining a distinctly math-like activity? Outlines require disciplined thought about relationships and force you to be organized. If you are using outlining as a study aid, you don't have to use the strict format. You can be flexible, using a convenient form that is modified to suit the information.

The information below is presented first in paragraph, and then in a modified outline form to illustrate how much more comprehensible the information becomes when presented in outline form:

> The three most commons ways of finding the prime factorization of a number are to factor the number in any way possible at first and then continue factoring until all of the factors are prime numbers, use a factor tree, or perform successive divisions until only prime numbers are the divisors.

In modified outline form, this information could look like this:

> Three ways to find the prime factors of a number:
> 1. Factor in any possible way at first and then keep factoring until you have only prime numbers.
> 2. Use a factor tree.
> 3. Do successive division.

The modified outline form makes it so much easier to see parallel relationships, such as three ways to accomplish the same thing.

Paraphrasing: Reword and Regroup

Another communication skill is paraphrasing, which means to reword and regroup. When we can express something in our own words, we know we understand it. However, what words are we allowed to replace in a paraphrase? It is *not* advisable to replace the technical words of math. For example:

> Multiply the fraction by 1 using n/n. If a specific denominator is desired, choose n by determining the number the original denominator should be multiplied by in order to get the desired denominator.

In paraphrasing this, we should not replace technical mathematical terms like *multiply, fraction,* or *denominator*. But we can do something like this:

> I need to multiply the fraction by 1 using n/n. If I'm looking for a specific denominator, I need to figure out what number the original denominator should be multiplied by to get the denominator I want.

To summarize, if we want students to become better readers of the texts of mathematics, we need to break the process of reading mathematics down into *before, during,* and *after* phases, and explicitly teach (explain and model, give practice time) strategies that apply to each phase.

What Kinds of Reading?

Reading Explanations in the Mathematics Textbook

In most cases, the mathematics textbook is used for two reasons: as a guide to reinforce, review, and supplement instruction and as a source for practice problems. When students have a teacher who understands how the mathematics textbook can strengthen learning, they can learn more than the mathematics in the textbook—they can learn how to use *any* textbook efficiently to help them.

Let's look at the features of the mathematics textbook, thinking about those features as ways to access and reinforce understandings as the school year progresses. Typically, a the mathematics textbook has these features:

- Table of Contents
- Pictures
- Charts, graphs, diagrams
- Lists of definitions
- Chapter overviews
- Explanations
- Practice Problems
- Examples
- "Connections"
- End-of-chapter material:
  - Summaries and reviews
  - Cumulative quizzes

In my workshops for reading in the content areas, I usually ask teachers to describe the relationship that the students are expected to have with the textbook: How does your textbook fit into your course? What are students expected to do with it? Are students expected to derive new information from the textbook? Use it in class? Have it open most of the time? Does the instruction follow along with the textbook? Will the textbook help them when they've missed class due to absence? Will the textbook clarify what they may not have understood in your instruction? To what extent do the practice problems in the textbook match your quizzes and tests? Does the textbook provide appropriate practice sets?

For some reason, many teachers look at their feet when asked these questions. Others stiffen up and declare: "We don't use a textbook," or "We hate our textbook." OK, but the textbook offers knowledge about the language of mathematics. Whatever we may think of the textbook, that textbook, even a not-so-good one, can provide very useful information and background for a particular mathematics course. The textbook is bound to be replete with mathematics language arranged in an organized way.

What follows are several learning models whose purpose is to acquaint students with the language and organization of their textbook. These lessons are predicated on the fact that background knowledge is the key to reading comprehension. Background knowledge comes in slowly but surely—it is absorbed, not installed. These learning experiences familiarize the students with any new language that they are about to encounter, review recently learned language, and reconnect the student to known language and concepts to prepare the mind for related information.

I'm looking at a mathematics textbook designed for middle school students. It is Carrafiello's *Pre-Algebra* (1997), and it has the standard features of books of its kind. It's reader-friendly to the eye, with ample white space, lots of boxes and shaded areas to mark off examples, marginal notes to help the student solve problems, and it includes photographs (albeit in humble black and white) to encourage students to anchor the mathematics concepts in real-life situations, especially sports. Although it was written more than a decade ago, the information and format of this textbook is probably typical of the one in your classroom right now. Mathematics textbooks haven't changed that much.

Getting to Know the Textbook: The Table of Contents

I don't know how many mathematics teachers do explicit lessons on the table of contents in the early days of the school year, but it's a good idea. Taking students through the table of contents lays the foundation for the language (and key concepts represented by that language) that they are about to encounter. Instead of having the students hear the language for the first time when they reach a particular chapter later in the year, why not give those terms a head start?

But you can't just have students staring at the table of contents. They need to engage it in some way. The purpose of the engagement is simply to familiarize themselves with the topics and terms. Let's take a look at Unit One of the *Pre-Algebra* book:

Unit One
    Chapter 1
    Review of Whole Numbers
    1.1 Place Value
    1.2 Comparing Numbers
    1.3 Rounding
    1.4 Addition
    1.5 Subtraction

1.6 Estimating Sums and Differences
1.7 Multiplication
1.8 Using Exponents
1.9 Division
1.10 Estimating Products and Quotients
1.11 Calculator: Performing Operations
1.12 Problem Solving: Guess, Check, and Revise
1.13 Application: Perimeter
Chapter Review

As stated, this chapter is a review. That means that the student is expected to be somewhat familiar with its information. But summer vacation has its way of washing academic information away like waves on the sand, so we shouldn't be surprised at the blank stares we get when we ask students on the first day of school what they know about exponents. As a formative assessment, we can have students express how well they think they know the topics in the chapter headings. They can express the depth of their knowledge about each chapter heading in a continuum or by color coding. (Items that are completely unfamiliar are to be highlighted in pink; items that are somewhat familiar are to be highlighted in blue; items that are very familiar are to be highlighted in green.) That would give you valuable information about who needs what kind of review to bring everyone up to speed for the new school year. With time at a premium, you don't want to be spending more time than necessary on Chapter 1.

Chapter 2 introduces the new information for the course:

Chapter 2
Number Expressions, Equations, and Properties
    2.1 Number Expressions
    2.2 Simplifying Number Expressions
    2.3 Expressions with Parentheses
    2.4 Equivalent Number Expressions
    2.5 Number Equations
    2.6 Addition Properties
    2.7 Multiplication Properties
    2.8 Other Properties
    2.9 Calculator: Simplifying Expressions
    2.10 Problem Solving: Numbers for Words
    2.11 Application: Area
    Chapter Review
Unit One Review

Remember, the purpose of this perusal of the table of contents is not to define any terms, just to begin to create familiarity with the language of the textbook. We can ask:

- What words do we already know, outside of a mathematics context?
- What do we think of when we hear the words *expression, properties*?
- Are any words unfamiliar? Do any of the unfamiliar words look like familiar words?

Unit Two
Chapter 3
Variable Expressions
    3.1 Variable Expressions
    3.2 Like Terms
    3.3 Combining Like Terms
    3.4 Evaluating Variable Expressions
    3.5 Using More Operations
    3.6 Using More Variables
    3.7 Calculator: Evaluating Expressions
    3.8 Problem Solving: Draw a Picture
    3.9 Application: Volume
    Chapter Review

- What words do we already know, outside of a mathematical context?
- What do we think of when we hear the words *expression, properties*?
- Are any words unfamiliar? Do any of the unfamiliar words look like familiar words?
- What patterns are we seeing in these three chapters? That is, what do all three chapters have in common?
- What words in Chapter 3 are carryovers from Chapter 2?

Chapter 4
Variable Equations
    4.1 Variable Equations
    4.2 Equivalent Equations
    4.3 Properties of Equality
    4.4 Inverse Operations

4.5 Solving Equations by Subtracting
4.6 Solving Equations by Adding
4.7 Solving Equations by Multiplying
4.8 Solving Equations by Dividing
4.9 Using More than One Operation
4.10 Calculator: Checking Solutions
4.11 Problem Solving: Number Patterns
4.12 Application: Solving Formulas

And again, we are asking the same questions about familiar words, unfamiliar words, unfamiliar words having familiar sounds/appearances, words that carry over from the previous chapter. If students are hearing, seeing, and saying the words of the table of contents, they are taking the very first steps into developing background knowledge. Although it may seem unnecessary or even inadvisable to have students say words whose meanings they are not learning immediately, doing so is actually valuable because it lays the groundwork for exploration of these terms when the time comes.

Poor readers tend not to look at the inside of polysyllabic words. They may read the words *equation* and *expression* as the same. They need repeated exposure to the sounds and appearances of these words.

It would be boring to have the students listen passively to you reading off the headings in the table of contents. Some teachers have the class toss a beach ball to each other to take turns reading. Others use choral reading—whole class, just the girls, just the boys, just the left side of the room, just the right side of the room. The point is to allow the students to have fun with the language, give it a rhythm, make them associate the words with a positive classroom experience. Building familiarity with the language helps to counteract the negative force known as math anxiety.

Do the Math on the Table of Contents

The table of contents itself can form the basis of a mathematics lesson.

- How many units do we have? What is the average number of pages in each unit?

- How many chapters do we have? How many headings do we have in each chapter? What is the average number of headings in each chapter? What is the estimated number of pages devoted to each heading?

- Considering the length of the school year, how much time would we be able to devote to each unit? Each chapter? Each heading? Create a calendar that disperses the topics evenly over the course of the school year. Do we have enough time? What can we do if we don't? If we have extra time, what should we do with it, mathwise?

Chapter Overviews

Before digging in to the topics in a chapter, it's advisable to lead the class in an overview of the chapter. The purpose of the overview is to familiarize students with the language, illustrations, and concepts that they are about to learn. This familiarity will facilitate learning when the concepts are introduced formally.

Three Gears of Prereading: Skimming, Scanning, Sampling

Most mathematics textbooks are well organized. Chapters may open with a list of learning objectives followed by a list of new mathematical vocabulary. Give students a few minutes to page through the chapter, name that reading mode as "skimming" and give them a purpose for their skimming: "Skim the chapter, getting a feel for how long it is and what kinds of problems we'll be learning how to solve." After students have skimmed the chapter, assure them that they will be able to solve the problems with your help.

After skimming, it's time to scan the chapter for specific information. The difference between skimming and scanning is that skimming is getting a bird's eye view of the reading territory, and scanning is swooping down to grab the specific information that we had our eyes peeled to find. Ask students to scan the chapter for a particular mathematical term like "associative property." Or, ask them to scan the chapter for particular mathematical task verbs, such as "simplify." *How many times in this chapter are you going to be asked to simplify?*

The next gear of reading is sampling. Theoretically, we're supposed to ask students to find a segment of text that looks interesting to them and have them read it. Honestly, mathematics textbooks are not usually written in a way that draws the interest of most students. So, we're going to have to tweak the question to get students to sample part of the chapter:

- Find something in this chapter that you already know about.
- Find something in this chapter that reminds you of something in another class or outside of school.
- Find something in this chapter that you can explain in your own words.

Think about how ready students would be to process the information in the chapter if they spent just one class period overviewing the text by skimming, scanning, and sampling. Because you've invested time in these prereading activities, the students have a much better chance of absorbing the new language and concepts than if you jumped right in.

The other two gears of reading informational text are reading and studying. By reading, we mean reading every word for full information. But this is prepared reading, reading that has already been informed and fortified by the background knowledge gleaned from the skimming, scanning, and sampling. By studying, we mean rereading, even memorizing. But it isn't mindless memorization; it's memorizing key concepts anchored in meaning and understanding. As we all know, competency in mathematics requires a certain amount of memorization.

Reading the Explanations in the Mathematics Textbooks:

Typically, mathematics textbooks set forth key explanations in straightforward language at the outset of the topic heading, like this:

Variable Expressions

A variable is a letter that represents any number in a mathematical expression.
Examples of Variable Expressions:

$x - y$ $\qquad\qquad$ $t + 4$ $\qquad\qquad$ $8 - c + d$

As you can see, this explanation assumes that the student understands other mathematical terminology: *represents, expression.*

Achieving Speed and Accuracy as a Reader of Mathematics

Everyone gets better at reading by reading. And that refers to *any* kind of reading. The habitual reader builds speed, accuracy, vocabulary, and cultural knowledge. Let's see why each of these qualities applies to mathematical performance.

Speed

Given the mind's ability to hold only a finite amount of information in short-term memory, it makes sense that slow readers are at a serious disadvantage. By the time they lumber through a sentence or paragraph, they have forgotten how it began. For readers to make and retain meaning from text, they need to process text quickly. Slow readers also suffer from test anxiety because when you fear that you don't have enough time you generate the kind of stress that robs concentration.

Speed is built through practice, yes, but there's more strategy to it than that. People who read (with comprehension) fast are skilled groupers of words. They read phrases, not single words. They can do this because they recognize language patterns that appear in certain kinds of text. The language of mathematics relies heavily on the same phrases and phraseology that appear over and over again. In other words, the language of mathematical definitions, word problems, and mathematical relationships follow a familiar pattern. Readers who recognize the patterns of mathematical language can process multiple words at one glance. Let's take a closer look at that:

We can teach students how to read their mathematics textbooks more quickly and efficiently by training them to recognize the language patterns and word groupings of mathematics. To illustrate exactly what this means, let's look at the word groupings that are typical of an end-of-year eighth grade high-stakes assessment:

- Greatest common factor
- Congruent angles; complementary angles
- Coordinate grid
- Best estimate
- Scale map
- Pairs of angles
- The sum of a number and its square
- A relationship between x and y
- Pythagorean theorem

Most children in the primary grades are taught how to read using a combination of methods. Let's look at these methods and extrapolate them to reading mathematics textbooks in the later grades: phonemic awareness.

Accuracy

The inaccurate reader misreads unfamiliar multisyllabic words because she pays attention to the beginnings and ends of words. The middle gets lost. Consequently, the inaccurate reader tends to mistake words pairs like the following:

- coordinate, cooperate

- perpendicular, particular
- geometric, geographic
- combination, competition
- representation, reputation
- protractor, projector
- expression, exposition
- millimeter, milliliter
- percentage, parentage

In most of the above word pairs, the first word only refers to mathematics; the second word in the pair (for the most part) is a word that would be found in another subject area (e.g., *geographic, exposition*), or general conversation (e.g., *particular, reputation*). You might think that it is a student's recognition of the math-specific words only that is relevant to mathematical performance. But unless the student has frequent contact—through reading—with the other words, how can she be expected to discriminate between a word that *looks like* a mathematical word? The point is that many key mathematical words look like other words that would be unfamiliar—therefore easily confused—with these key mathematical words. So, if I'm teaching mathematics, I want my students to know, upon sight, that the word *competition* is not the word *combination*.

Both speed and accuracy in reading are developed through practice—practice in *any* kind of reading. The mathematics teacher who thinks that a schoolwide sustained silent reading initiative is for the "other teachers," does not understand the concept of investment. As with money well invested, time well invested yields more than the original capital. Time in school invested into reading will result in greater speed and accuracy when it comes to mathematics reading. The improvements in speed and accuracy pay off in the student's ability to devote more energy to the actual mathematics to be extracted from the text.

Vocabulary and Cultural Knowledge

Looking at a state assessment for seventh grade mathematics, I see the following cultural references:

- subzero weather in January
- St. Cloud, Minnesota
- elevation in Antarctica
- painting a room

- carnival rides
- a planter (container for growing plants, not a person who plants)
- a customer service department
- a software company
- the orbits of Jupiter's moons

These are not mathematical terms. Yet, terms like these are mentioned in the setups of the mathematics questions on this state assessment. Now, you could argue that a student could figure the mathematics correctly without knowing what these ambient words mean. You could also argue that general knowledge will not solve mathematical problems. But a student who does know the cultural referents that pop up in mathematical problems is at a distinct advantage because the problem seems more real and because it will be easier to employ one's mathematical intuition to a known situation than in a vacuum.

Conclusion

I'm hoping that, as a result of reading this chapter, you understand your role in incorporating good reading strategies and reinforcing productive reading habits in the service of teaching mathematics. I'm hoping that you see that the time you spend on these strategies and habits is time well invested. And I'm hoping that you recognize that reading comprehension is highly genre based. Let's use a sports metaphor: While a certain set of skills (speed, hand–eye coordination, agility, focus, strength) is applicable to all sports, you would not ask a hockey coach to coach basketball. You, when you are teaching mathematics, are the specific coach for the type of reading that students are expected to do *in mathematics.*

STRATEGY 4

Teaching Mathematics with Metaphor and Gesture

Excellent teachers of mathematics use plain English to teach through imagery, simple metaphors and consistent gestures. Metaphor—explaining one thing in terms of another—is simultaneously one of the most basic and most sophisticated ways of thinking. Metaphors are almost always visual. When metaphors and imagery are accompanied with gesture, the depth of learning and durability of memory are strengthened.

To understand and manipulate an abstract concept, we need to mentally translate it into a concrete image. The more familiar we are with the abstract concept, the faster it is for us to mentally do abstract-to-concrete translation, and the less we even realize we are doing it. When we become thoroughly competent on the abstract concept, we forego the concrete translation and are able to operate within the abstract model. A simple example is to use a set of scales to represent an equation: any change to one side affects the other.

Getting students to think visually and metaphorically about mathematical concepts begins early in their education. They learn to count items, group them into items that will be thought of as units, and then count the units. They learn to read and write numbers through the visual, metaphorical model of place value. Let's consider the difference between a child who learns only the algorithm for addition and subtraction with "carrying and borrowing" as opposed to the child who understands the process of addition and subtraction through the metaphor of "regrouping."

Mandy is a third grader who has learned to recite an internal monologue when she adds columns of numbers. As she adds 17 + 25, she'll say to herself: "I line up my numbers. 7 plus 5 is 12. You can't fit 12 into the ones column, so I bring down my 2, carry my 1. Now I add my 1, plus 1, plus 2, equals 4, and my answer is 42." Mandy is becoming competent in multidigit addition. However, Mandy does not understand the concept of place value that undergirds the process.

♦ 41

Marissa, a third grader in another class, has learned the concept of grouping and regrouping by using manipulatives, first through ice cream sticks and then through coins. Although she understands the concepts, she has difficulty doing the multidigit addition and subtraction.

In both cases—in the absence of manipulatives (Mandy's memorized procedure only) and in the presence of manipulatives (Marissa's conceptual understanding only)—what the students need is language to create the bridge from concrete to abstract. This bridge can be created through the language of metaphor. "Metaphor use has many benefits. These include understanding difficult ideas and representations, improving memory, computing and detecting and correcting errors" (Chiu, p. 1).

The theory of constructivism posits that learning does not arise full-bodied like Athena from the head of Zeus, but rather, learning is built, brick by brick, from an existing foundation (schema). Metaphorical learning taps into schema. Students come to us with knowledge about nonmath topics, such as *a container*. The student, I'll call him Stephen, understands a lot about containers (boxes, bags, envelopes, etc.), so when he begins to learn about variables, he can understand them in terms of containers: A variable is a container. In it is a quantity. Just as the contents of a container can be exchanged for different contents, the quantity represented by a variable can be changed, exchanged, interchanged. Stephen understands the concept of how a traveler moves through a path. A variable may also be understood in terms of a traveler: Just as a traveler is at a given location at a particular time, that same traveler will be at a different location at another time. An unknown variable can be thought of as a traveler with an unknown location; a known variable can be thought of as a traveler with a known location. The efficacy of any metaphor depends upon (a) the extent of familiarity with the source (containers, travelers, scales) and (b) the extent of the match between the source and the target (new information).

Therefore, it's best to keep your metaphors simple. Containers are effective because they are entirely familiar, there are different kinds of them, and containers can have small compartments within them. Traveling is an effective metaphor because it is entirely familiar and connects with roads, branching roads, entrances and exits on roads, packing, having a home base, being the same person in different locations, etc. (Excuse the pun: we can get a lot of mileage out of the traveler metaphor.) Scales are an effective metaphor because you can see what happens to the balance when either side is given more weight than the other or when weight is removed. Trees are an effective metaphor: trees have roots, branches and leaves; trees change with the seasons; trees produce fruit or flowers; other living things make their homes in trees. An ecosystem, such as a river, is an effective metaphor: a river flows to a larger entity, the sea; rivers sustain life; rivers have banks and beds (sides and bases). A family is an effective metaphor: families are units formed with similar members; there's a nuclear family of closely related members and an extended family of more distantly related members; families tend to work toward a common purpose. And a team is an effective metaphor: members of teams wear the same uniform; team members form a replacement set for one another; teams work toward a common purpose.

A model for teaching with metaphors is a three-step process:

1. Get students thinking about the features of the source. Show students a simple and familiar object, such as a box. Ask them to say everything they know about an egg carton, keeping the conversation on an entirely literal level. This establishes your starting point. It also piques students' curiosity and makes them feel secure: *Why are we talking about egg cartons? Why are we saying such obvious things about something so simple as an egg carton? I don't know where this is going, but it seems easy.*

2. Elicit the known math-like language from the students and write the relevant words and phrases on the board: *container, compartments, units, single, interchangeable, exchange....*

3. Introduce the math concept by incorporating as much of the known language as possible and transitioning into the math language. In effect, we are saying to the students: "You already understand the concepts. We're just shifting into applying that familiar concept into the math world now."

Mrs. G uses egg cartons and dried beans to teach place value. She cuts up the egg carton into two-compartment units to teach how double-digit numbers represent tens and ones. The students learn that they can't "fit" more than nine beans into the ones's compartment. This is how they begin to understand the need for regrouping. To teach three-digit numbers, Mrs. G cuts the egg cartons into three-compartment units, and the students have to explain what the numbers mean, using the language of place value.

When it comes time to learn use regrouping in addition and subtraction, Mrs. G uses the egg carton metaphor by cutting the carton into six-compartment units. By viewing the half-dozen carton vertically, she has spaces for two two-digit numbers and the sum or difference, respectively. She guides the students from the concrete (egg carton) model to the symbolic (numeral and symbol) model by using language. *Compartments* become columns, the act of moving beans from one compartment to another becomes *regrouping*. The experience of having used, seen, and talked about the beans in the egg carton compartments helps students concretize and understand the abstraction.

Here is how metaphorical teaching of math is described by Ming Ming Chiu: The target math to be taught is the concept of zero, numbers, absolute value, etc. The teacher, whom I will call Mrs. L, wants to use the metaphor of traveling on a street. But first, she has to know that the children understand the source, which would be the relevant characteristics of a street: starting point, street signs, landmarks, sidewalks, traffic signals, etc. Mrs. L gets the children thinking about the (metaphorical) source by mapping out a little street journey represented by a line on the white board. She tells a story about beginning at her house (marked on the line as the midpoint), traveling east, traveling west. The story is thoroughly comprehensible *because the children understand the source.* Mrs. L then retells the same little story, this time renaming the key concepts with math language: The address of her house (starting point on the number line) is zero; points traveling east are positive numbers; points west, negative. Through this simple metaphor, the children understand the target math by cashing in, so to speak, their understanding of the source (the street). To put the concept of metaphorical teaching in fancier terms: The students "project source properties and actions on to the target math" (Chiu, p. 4). That is to say, if the student can answer questions about the source (talking about traveling on the street), then they can answer parallel questions about the target math. It's a matter of switching from familiar language to mathematical language.

A number line is a common metaphor that allows us to visualize relationships between numbers. Number lines are particularly useful when it comes to explaining negative numbers. You know how difficult it is to get some students to truly understand the concept of negative numbers. We often explain how negative numbers work by referring to the thermometer, money debts, and the number line.

Before we continue, I want to remind you of the KISS (*Keep It Simple, Sweetheart*) principle of teaching through metaphor: The metaphor is going to work only if it is simple enough for the students to understand the source. The beauty of teaching through metaphor is that the student is, at first, saying "Why are we doing this? This is so simple?" Where are we going with this? Gradually, you introduce the language of the target math, progressively shifting your language in accordance with the students' understanding.

The metaphor works like training wheels on a bicycle. Before the rider knows it, the training wheels are gone. In this case, before the students know it, they are talking about math without the metaphorical source. That is what experts do: experts don't need the metaphorical training wheels anymore. "In short…students can learn math by making sense of the source, describing their work with everyday language and then learning the math language" (Chiu, p. 5).

Metaphorical reasoning connects and expands mathematical ideas, improves retrieval, and even facilitates construction of new math concepts.

Analyzing Well-Known Math Metaphors

Metaphors are powerful, but they don't have to be a perfect fit. We take them as far as they can go to illuminate meaning. Metaphors establish common ground between two things, but we need to keep in mind that there is outlying ground between these two things as well. Metaphorical thinking fails when the limits of the metaphor are not observed. For example, the term *fact family* is a convenient and effective metaphor. A fact family is defined as a number sentence about addition, subtraction, multiplication, or division. Each number sentence in the fact family has the same numbers:

$7 + 4 = 11$

$4 + 7 = 11$

$11 - 4 = 7$

$11 - 7 = 4$

The metaphor of a family fits in that members of a family go together and are somewhat the same. Of course, family members are not exactly different versions of the *exact* same elements, as in the set that we call *fact families*.

Another imperfect but useful metaphor is thinking of any equation as a *sentence*. The metaphor works because an equation, like a sentence, expresses a kind of complete thought. An equation has two sides, just like a sentence having a subject and a predicate. However, the relationship between the subject and predicate in a grammatical sentence is quite different from the relationship represented by both sides of an equation. Nevertheless, applying the familiar term *sentence* to describe a two-sided relationship in the math world makes sense, is memorable, and is enlightening.

A *factor tree* is a metaphor that works to display (and thus illuminate) the prime factorization of a number. The heart of the metaphor is that the factor tree appears to have branches. However, unlike an actual tree, when you create a factor tree you start at the top and branch your way down, broadening the tree as you go.

There is a difference between a representation, such as a graph or chart, and a metaphor. With metaphor, you have two things, each having its own reality. A representation, such as a bar graph, however, does not have a life outside its use as a representation of a specific thing. A bar graph is a representation, not a metaphor. A circle graph is called so because it is a circle, not a metaphor for a circle. A pie chart is a metaphor. It is not a pie. It looks like one and is sliced like one. What metaphors and representations do have in common is that they both use another model to illuminate meaning.

Below is a list of concepts and how you might explain them through metaphor:

Concept	Metaphor	Explanation
What is an algorithm?	A recipe	An algorithm, like a recipe, gives you step-by-step directions. We use algorithms to do procedures like long division.
What is the commutative property of addition?	People on a train	Let's say you have five women and seven men on a train, a total of twelve people. It doesn't matter where they are sitting. It doesn't matter if you count the seven men first and the five women second or the other way around. That is how the commutative property of addition works. It doesn't matter the order in which you add whatever you are adding together. Any order of addition will give you the same result.
What is the commutative property of multiplication?	Egg carton	There are a dozen compartments in an egg carton. Six lengthwise, two widthwise. Whether you multiply six by two or two by six, you still get twelve every time. That is how the commutative property of multiplication works.
What is the distributive property?	Kiss from mother to her children	Think of the number outside the parentheses as the mother of the numbers within the parentheses. The mother "gives a kiss" to *each* of the children!
What is the associative property?	Groupings of people at a party	When you think of how the associative property works, think of how people act at a party. They mingle, going from group to group. But still, you have the same amount of people at the party, no matter how they decide to group themselves.
What is a variable?	Your wardrobe	A variable is something that can be changed, just like your clothing. Think of the variable as being like your shirt: replaceable by any number of other shirts. When you solve for a variable, that is like deciding which particular shirt you are going to wear.

It may be hard to tell a metaphor from an application of a concept. For example, we can illustrate the meaning of ordered pair by using a road map. We find the location of a given city on the map by using two coordinates on the horizontal and vertical axes in accordance with the index provided by the mapmaker. But is the literal road map a metaphor for what we mean by ordered pairs, or is it an ordered pair simply put to use for a practical purpose?

The Math-as-Motion Metaphor

As described previously, Mrs. L used the metaphor of a street, with numbers metaphorically traveling in a positive or negative direction along that street. Now let's apply the math-as-motion metaphor to understanding how we compute the perimeter of a polygon by summing the lengths of all its sides. Pretend that you are walking along the lines that define the polygon. You start in Location A and then count each step until you end up at Location A again. If you were to use your own steps as the unit of measurement, the length of the perimeter would be the number of steps you took.

That is extremely simple and obvious, but let's see how, in staying with that simple metaphor of line-as-path/math-as-motion we can expand into new understandings:

> New target connections include…ordering all sides creates a preceding side and a following side for each side. Sum the lengths of adjacent sides. Maintain a partial sum….When recalling any of these pieces of information, the new connections provide more means to activate the remaining pieces of information. Thus, the likelihood of recalling the algorithm and all the related concepts increases. By creating additional meaningful connections, metaphorical reasoning can improve recall of math relationships. (Chiu, p. 6)

Using Gestures to Clarify Metaphors and Meaning

Get your hands into the math! According to a study cited in *Science Daily* (May, 2007), teachers in Hong Kong and Japan use gestures more than American teachers do as a cognitive support for explanations of mathematical concepts. When images and gestures are used along with analogies, the study finds, the concepts are learned with more durability.

> US teachers incorporate analogies into their lessons as often as teachers in Hong Kong and Japan, but they less frequently utilize a spatial supports, mental and visual imagery, and gestures that encourage active reasoning. Less cognitive support may result in

> students retaining less information, learning less in a conceptual way, or misunderstanding the analogies. (*Science News*, 2007)

This book emphasizes the importance of language in the teaching of math, but gesture is a natural part of language. "Gesture promotes learning....Children are more likely to profit from instruction when it includes gesture than when it does not" (Cook & Goldin-Meadow, 2006, p. 227). Gesture clarifies language and improves the likelihood that the language will be remembered. Moreover, the learner who views gesture accompanying the teacher's language is likely to imitate those gestures.

Gesture is important for learning for a variety of reasons. When we fortify language with gesture, we engage the spatial, visual, and kinesthetic neural pathways. Gesture can consolidate related information in a problem, allowing the learner to distinguish between important and secondary information. Another benefit of gestures is that if the same gesture is repeated from problem to problem, the learner begins to focus on common elements between problems. For example, the concept that both sides of an equation are the same and that actions done to one side must be counteracted on the other side can be communicated with a sweeping gesture. When a student sees that sweeping gesture repeated in several problems involving equations, she will draw connections among the problems: All have equations; in an equation, both sides are the same and actions done to one side must be counteracted on the other side.

Gestures can represent abstract ideas. "There is increasing evidence that embodied forms of representation are involved in cognitive processes, including working memory, mental imagery, action memory, and linguistic processing....Gesture, as an embodied representational format, could preferentially engage any one or all of these four systems in contributing to learning" (Cook & Goldin-Meadow, 2006, p. 229).

What we want is for students to produce the gestures themselves, tying gesture to language and concept. There is evidence to support the theory that producing a gesture "reduces the load on working memory systems; speakers remember more items...when they gesture while explaining a math problem than when they do not gesture" (Cook & Goldin-Meadow, 2006, p. 228). Use of gesture with speech frees up cognitive space that can be used for reflection and creation of new ideas. In other words, as the mind relies less on having to concentrate on the words of a message they are trying to convey, the mind is free to think deeper thoughts!

When we perform an action (gesture), we enhance our memory for that action. In other words, we tend to remember what we act out. That is why

> Hearing signers remember action phrases that they have signed better than action phrases that they have said....Similarly, deaf signers remember action phrases that they have signed as well

> as action phrases that they have enacted, and both are better remembered than action phrases that were merely read. (Cook & Goldin-Meadow, 2006, p. 229)

This finding supports our conclusion that language and gesture are a powerful team to facilitate learning.

Gesturing itself, along with the language that it represents, facilitates accessing of the concept in the brain. In other words, if we've learned the language with an accompanying gesture, we are more efficient at retrieving the information. This could be because the linguistic–gesture combination results in the creation of and memory for a mental image; that is, the production of a gesture results in the production of an image. The language–gesture–image formation solidifies the learning and facilitates its retrieval.

Finally, gesture production embedded in language helps to create the mental models necessary for understanding math. "[G]esture production encourages more developed and more accurate mental models of the problem and concept, sustaining deeper learning" (Cook & Goldin-Meadow, 2006, p. 229).

Used repeatedly, the gestures associated with language gradually blends with the language to form meaning. That is to say, at first, the gestures may not hold meaning. But as the student blends language and gesture in a supportive learning environment, meaning is absorbed. According to the Cook and Goldin-Meadow study, "when children first learn a task the gestures they produce may not be fully imbued with meaning. It may be only in the continued doing that these gestures take on their full meaning" (2006, p. 5).

Graphic Representations as Metaphor

Popular graphic representations of mathematical concepts represent one thing (a mathematical concept) in terms of another (a diagram).

The metaphor that the Venn diagram relies upon is that *sets are containers*. In a Venn diagram in which one circle (Set A) is encased inside a larger circle (Set B), we are representing that Set A is a subset of Set B.

In her book, *Creative Graphing* (1986), Marji Freeman shares her techniques in "taking mathematics out of the textbook and putting it into real-life situations" (p. 3). Freeman takes the approach of using interesting, relevant information as the subject of graphs.

Freeman's kid-friendly way of inviting students into the graphing world strengthens the language of sets: more, most, less, least, fewer, the majority of, trend, appears to be leaning toward, preponderance of, increasing, decreasing, diminishing, growing, number of, amount, intersection of, overlapping, set, members of the set of, outliers, union, complement, region, disjoint, conjoint, correspondence, element, universal set, subset, empty set, null set, contained, cardinality, percent, proportion, relation, relationship, ratio, data, analyze, analysis, interpret, interpretation, results, vertical axis, horizontal axis, approximate, approximately.

Some of these words are quite sophisticated, certainly not already in the vocabulary of an elementary school student. However, by using consistent gestures and parallel language (using the mathematical language accompanied by familiar language), the skillful teacher can make these new words comprehensible, or can at least introduce them into the students' schema.

> Set notation ($\neq$, $\leq$, $\geq$, $<$, $=$, $>$, { }, etc.) looks foreign and can therefore be intimidating. But the graphic representations, while "saying" the same thing as the symbolic representations, are more comprehensible because, unlike the symbols, they are metaphorical. Here's where we can understand the difference between a mathematical symbol and a graphic metaphor. A mathematical symbol does not have its own meaning apart from its function to "do its job" in math, but a graphic metaphor, such as a box, grid, or circle, represents a *container* or *system of containers*.

Freeman suggests ways to engage students in the language of math as they learn to understand what the graphs mean: "I have found that most students have difficulty understanding a Venn Diagram at first. If this is new for your students, discuss what the interesting circles mean before the students are to respond on a graph" (Freeman, 1986, p. 7).

Using the class itself as the universal set, Freeman had the students graph their own opinions and experiences. She then prompted them to interpret and explain what they saw on the graphs, posing questions like:

- What do we know about the members of our class by looking at our graph?
- What different kinds of _____ do we notice by looking at our graph?
- How many people prefer _____? How do we know?
- About what percent of the members of our class _____?
- About what fraction of the members of our class _____?
- Approximate the decimal that represents the number of _____.
- Which _____ is the most/least popular (common, frequent)?
- What does the information tell us about the ratio between boys and girls on this issue?
- Express the information about our class in a complete sentence.

- Explain the information about our class in a well-developed paragraph.
- What, if anything, surprises you about the results of our graph? Why?
- What, if anything, could you have predicted about the results of our graph? Why?

Freeman's students processed the information on the graphs through language. "The most important part of using graphs in the classroom is to process them thoroughly. It is from this exploration that students have the opportunity to examine the data, analyze the information, and interpret the results" (1986, p. 6). Students responded to class-directed questions in the traditional raise-your-hand-and-answer fashion; but, I think more importantly, they discussed the graphs in small groups, in think-pair-share partnerships, and in writing.

Figure 4.1 shows how a Venn diagram would work to display an array of preferences about a class trip.

Figure 4.1. Venn Diagram

Where would you like to go on a class trip?

Students are asked to write their initials or place a sticky note representing their preference. The Venn diagram structure allows students to express just how strongly they feel about a particular choice, whether they are torn between two choices, or even whether they are neutral.

The students are asked to write their initials, or place a marker, on the Venn diagram in a place that indicates their preference, or an overlap of preferences. Students who feel very strongly in favor of one of the three choices can write their initials or markers on the circumference; those who are more flexible, or are split between two preferences can write their initials or markers in the overlapping areas. They can even express neutrality by placing their initials in the center.

Once the students have written their initials or markers on the Venn diagram, the math begins. Students then are asked to describe, both in words and in numbers, the results of the survey. They can also be prompted by specific questions, such a those above.

If we ask students about their television-watching preferences, we incite a lively discussion. Freeman suggests the graph below (Figure 4.2) to harness such a discussion into a math problem. As with the Venn diagram, multiple interpretations are possible, leading to an opportunity to differentiate. A problem calling for more sophisticated analysis might call for extrapolation or disaggregation; a less sophisticated problem may call for just counting and doing simple totals and comparisons.

Figure 4.2. Class Graph 1

If you could watch TV only one night a week, which night would you choose?

Sunday	
Monday	
Tuesday	
Wednesday	
Thursday	
Friday	
Saturday	

Figure 4.3 shows another quantitative graph. This structure allows students to, by placement of their markers, show a range within each category. It may happen that the categories have to be recalibrated after seeing the results.

Figure 4.3. Class Graph 2

How many text messages do you send/receive per day?

More than twenty	Between six and nineteen
Fewer than five	None

Marji Freeman's *Creative Graphing*, is, unfortunately, out of print, but if you can get your hands on a copy, you'll enjoy it. Freeman suggests having the class graph information about birthdays; family life; travel and experience; all kinds of favorite things, hobbies, and interests; even information about names (How many letters are in your first name? Last name? Do you have the letters XYZ in your name? Do you have a middle name? Were you named after someone? Does anyone else in the class share your first or last name?). She also suggests graphs that show the results of estimation by the students (length of a string, jelly beans in a jar, etc.). Students can be highly motivated to "do graphs" to find out about themselves in relation to their peers. However, we do need to be careful to protect their privacy and feelings and need to think carefully about, and even get a colleague's or parents' opinion, about certain issues that may be sensitive for some children. (Remember that most people—children especially—don't want to be seen as unusual when it comes to family and friends or physical attributes.)

Conclusion

I'm hoping that, as you've read this chapter, you've been thinking of the various ways in which you've been employing metaphors to teach math all along. You've been doing that intuitively because metaphors are natural and powerful ways of knowing. I'm hoping that you understand that, to be effective, metaphors have to be clear, and that clarity comes from simplicity. When it comes to teaching through metaphor, the most important thing is that the learner understand and feel comfortable with the source model (the thing on which the metaphor is based).

STRATEGY 5

Unlocking the Meaning of Word Problems

Excellent teachers of mathematics use plain English to give students strategies for unlocking the secrets of word problems. Actually, there are no "secrets" of word problems. Word problems must be read carefully. But many students have been led astray by unreliable shortcuts.

It hasn't helped as much as we might have thought to tell students to focus on a set of keywords that signal a particular operation. Just because words like *sum, in all, total of*, and *all* appear in a problem does not mean that we have to add! What we have to do is read the whole problem until we understand what it is asking us to do. Whether students have been (misleadingly) taught to look for key words that point to addition, subtraction, multiplication, or division in a problem, or whether they have figured out this "shortcut" for themselves, it is to be discouraged. A person designing a multiple-choice test is surely going to anticipate that some test takers are going to look for such key words and jump right into the wrong operation, coming up with a wrong answer that is right there waiting to trip up the hapless shortcut finder. Now wouldn't that be the oldest trick in the book? Of *course*, the key word is going to be misleading in at least some of the questions!

No getting around it: You have to read the problem carefully and then translate, as Dr. Concepcion Molina (2010) says, the English into math.

> Giselle had 2 liters of water. She drank 750 milliliters. How many milliliters of water does Giselle have left?
> A. 250
> B. 1,000
> C. 1,250
> D. 1,750

To solve this problem, the solver has to use language to translate the English into math: *I have to subtract, but I can't subtract quantities named in two dif-*

ferent units. I have to translate the liters into milliliters. That would be 2,000 milliliters that Giselle started out with: 2,000 − 750 = 1,250. (Check: 750 + 1,250 = 2,000).

Notice that I couldn't immediately jump from the original question right into the math. I had to interpret the question first (in words), and then translate the words into math. Thus, the cognitive procedure *before* the problem is in shape to be solved is:

1. Read the problem at least once.

2. Think about the demands of the problem.

3. Interpret the demands of the problem and express the demands of problem in words.

4. Translate the English into math

Dr. Molina urges teachers to coach students in how to reword the problem so that it is in position to be translated into math:

> "I have 2 numbers whose sum is 15. One of them is 8. What is the other number?" (Personal communication, Dec. 22, 2010.)

According to Molina, "A key is the translation and understanding of the context and to write it out in such a way so that the English statement can be translated into 'math.' So what a kid should do with the problem above is:

> "Write out 'one number plus another number is 15.' Translated to math this would be _____ + _____ = 15. Then the additional information tells you that one of those numbers is 8, so then logic dictates that the statement then becomes 8 + _____ = 15. Now you do what other plans tell you…solve and check for reasonableness and accuracy." (Personal communication, Dec. 22, 2010.)

Done this way, with language as the key strategy, the problem solves itself logically. No shortcuts. Just the use of language to mediate thought. (Maybe the reason why it works so well is that language happens to be the most powerful tool for thought that humans have. Hey, why not use it?) The shallow "look for the keywords" strategy is inaccurate, misleading, and likely to trick students into picking the wrong answer in a multiple choice question. After all, if you were designing a multiple choice question, wouldn't you try to tempt the unwary student with false keyword bait?

If the "look for the keyword strategy" fails for being too narrow, the "make a plan" strategy fails for being too broad. It's not that students are *not* supposed to make a plan to solve the problem. It's that simply telling them to do so is not very helpful (or strategic). Whatever plan is to go into effect has to be the result of first taming the language of the problem so that it can be translated into math!

So here we are again talking about the importance of language to understand mathematics. But it's not receptive language (listening, reading) alone. It's the productive (speaking, reading) functions of language that solvers must engage. To solve word problems, students have to talk and/or write to each other and to themselves.

An excellent way to get students to activate their internal monologue for problem solving is to do a think-aloud. A think-aloud differs from an explanation in that the think-aloud (as exemplified above, by Molina) is more informal and reveals the spontaneous thinking process. An explanation, on the contrary, is didactic and objective.

Background Knowledge and Mathematical Problems

Let's analyze the language of word problems. Most word problems have two kinds of language: language of mathematics and language of the context. Typical contexts include business transactions, sports, transportation, construction, cooking, and weather. Theoretically, you don't have to understand the context to solve the problem, but knowing about the context does help you decide whether an answer makes sense.

Below are several examples of problems about the stock market and finance:

> Example 1: During the course of one trading day, the price of a stock fluctuated between a high of $2 above the previous day's closing price and a low of $1.50 below the previous day's closing price. Calculate the difference between the high and low prices of that day.
>
> Example 2: On July 1 of this year, Ethan had $250.00 in his checking account. He withdraws $50 from his checking account every Monday. He deposits $60 every Tuesday. What is the balance in his checking account at the end of a two-month period?
>
> Example 3: The price of a stock increased $3 per day for a five-day period. If the stock continued to increase at that rate, what would be the total change in value in 20 days?

A student who does not know the words *fluctuate* and *previous* in the first problem and can't figure them out in this context is in trouble with this problem. But the student who doesn't know what *trading day* and *closing price* means is also in the dark not because she doesn't know the meaning of the individual words, but she is not familiar enough with the stock market (context of the problem) to know how familiar words are used in a specific context.

For the second problem, the student would have to know *withdraws, deposits,* and *balance,* not generically, but in the context of the problem, which is banking.

Imagine trying to solve the third problem without knowing anything about how the stock market words, including what a stock even is!

Now let's look some other problems, this time about a favorite context—football:

> Example 1: A football team lost 9 yards on each of three consecutive plays. What was the team's total change in position for the three plays?
>
> Example 2: A touchdown is worth 6 points. After a touchdown, a team can earn either 1 or 2 extra conversion points. A field goal is worth 3 points. A safety is worth 2 points. If a team scores 10 points, what are the possible combinations of touchdowns, conversions, field goals, and safeties?
>
> Example 3: A football team loses 5 yards on one play and then loses twice as many yards on the next play. Write an expression that represents the change in position after these two plays.

These problems can be solved by those (like me) who have never watched a football game, but they are easier to solve if you have. Knowing the context allows you to visualize the problem and that helps considerably. For a football fan, these three situations are immediately understandable. Background knowledge puts you at an advantage.

So if knowing about the context of word problems helps students solve them, and if students have very little background knowledge about the kinds of things word problems are about, how can we help? One way would be to engage students in conversations about business, sports, construction, cooking, and weather. In your skillful, teacherly way, steer those conversations into math territory. Before your students know it, they're solving problems!

The value of background knowledge in a variety of subjects affirms the importance of wide voluntary reading. When students read, good things happen in all subjects, and that does include mathematics. Wide voluntary reading expands background knowledge that can be relevant in math when students have to picture situations and make assumptions about whether a solution makes sense. It also improves comprehension and increases speed—two skills that are relevant to solving word problems.

Lack of background knowledge is the major impediment to reading comprehension and information processing in all academic areas, as all teachers find out. (Background knowledge is almost synonymous with vocabulary.)

The kind of background knowledge that students need for school success is the kind they will find in rich conversations that expand their world, and in the library. Drill, drill, drill on mathematical facts will go only so far to help a student solve a word problem about a context that the student knows nothing about. You can't turn your mathematics class into a reading factory. But you can be supportive of sustained silent programs that your school initiates. Sustained silent reading will help performance on word problems.

One way to engage students and get them to see the relevance of mathematics in their everyday lives is to have them make up their own word problems in a variety of contexts. Using the same template for a problem, students compose other scenarios.

> **Example: Multiplying Positive and Negative Fractions**
>
> Context: Food
> If 7/8 of the 140 calories in Marisa's favorite breakfast bar come from fat, how many calories come from fat?
>
> Context: Model building
> Jared is building a 1/9 scale model of a speedboat. If the propellers on the actual speedboat are 36 inches in diameter, what is the diameter of the propellers of the model?
>
> Context: Car trip
> Alexandra's car used 3/4 of a tank of gas to cross her state. The gas tank on her car holds 15.5 gallons. How many gallons of gas did it take to cross her state?

Choose five of the following contexts and write similar word problems:
- Cooking
- Basketball
- Bird flight
- Weightlifting
- Human body
- Yard work
- Decorating your room
- Things in your locker
- Vacations
- Pets

- Money
- Space

When Working with Students Individually

If your students are not ready to create their own full word problems, scaffold this task by providing cloze activities (sentences with blanks). This scaffolding activity is valuable because, to do a cloze activity, students have to understand and analyze the context to supply a word that can make sense in the blank.

You've seen visual acuity puzzles that show several pictures having slight differences. The solver is supposed to examine the pictures carefully and discern subtle differences, or to find two pictures that match exactly. You can do a similar thing with word problems to train students to read carefully and notice details. Given several versions of the same word problem, but with subtle differences in wording or punctuation, students have to notice the differences (or match two that are exact).

To build on existing skills, find a baseline word problem that a student can do and then turn up the heat on that problem, making it more complex by changing one detail at a time. You'll be able to calibrate where the student's competency breaks down and provide remediation accordingly.

A Cooperative Learning Strategy for Creating, Solving, and Evaluating Word Problems

In this modified jigsaw strategy, students are divided into four groups to write, strategize, solve, and evaluate their own word problems. Each group is given a photograph that represents some kind of action. For an excellent collection of high-quality, inexpensive photographs, I recommend a product called "Language Cards" manufactured by North Star Teacher Resources (2004). (I like these cards for their diversity, appeal to students, and durability.) The cards have nothing do to with math, per se, but the situations depicted on them can suggest all kinds of mathematical problems.

Every group is given one picture (or, you can distribute a few pics to each group, and have them decide which one to use). In Round One, each group is to compose a problem based on the picture. Obviously, mathematics must be used to solve the problem. Ideally, the problem should be solvable by using whatever concept is currently being learned. The written problem should involve the appropriate degree of sophistication, not just a simple question like, "How many this or that?" The problem must be clearly and legible written because it is about to be passed along to the next group.

In Round Two, the pictures along with their corresponding problems are passed around, clockwise. The task for each group is to write a procedure for solving the problem. (The task is not to solve the problem, only to write a procedure.)

In Round Three, the pictures, problems, and procedures are passed clockwise to the next group. The task is to solve the problem in strict adherence to the procedure that has been given. If the procedure will not result in the correct answer, the group has to follow it to the letter anyway, and pass it along for Round Four.

In Round Four, students check the answer. Then, the paperwork is returned to its original group for evaluation: How do the originators of the problem like the way it was handled? Is the procedure accurate and efficient? Has the answer been properly checked?

This modified jigsaw procedure is engaging and creative. It involves applying learned concepts by communication. Some teachers are concerned about the time it takes to do an activity such as this. However, it needn't take more than a single class period to do this. The time will be well worth it if students deepen their understandings of mathematics by communication.

You may be concerned about having one or two students do most of the work in each group while the others sit by. If this is the case, you can require everyone in the group to show their work.

Conclusion

I'm hoping that, after reading this chapter, you will teach students to do the intermediate step of translating word problems into mathematical language (translating English into math) before attempting to create a mathematical expression. I'm hoping, also, that you will get students to climb inside the language of word problems by writing their own, based on templates that represent problems for the topics.

STRATEGY 6

Teaching Note-Taking Skills for Mathematics

Excellent teachers of mathematics teachers use plain English to teach note-taking skills relevant to mathematical comprehension. They understand that note taking reinforces mathematical learning, but it is more than just copying from the board. A student's notes are a window to her thinking, forming those mental footprints on paper that break math down.

Excellent teachers actively teach and model note taking. They view time spent explicitly teaching note taking, in this case for mathematics, as time spent making students more proficient in the subject itself. Teaching how to learn the subject is inherent in teaching the subject.

Notes serve two purposes. The first is to help you focus as you listen. I call these *processing* notes. The second is to assist you in the future, such as when you need to study for a test or solve a problem. I call these *reminder* notes. Often, processing notes can be discarded; their purpose of ensuring concentration in the learner is fulfilled once the notes are written. Consequently, it might not matter if the notes are legible or even comprehensible. But reminder notes do have to be comprehensible to the learner later on. Orderly columns, legible handwriting, clearly labeled diagrams and steps are important.

Teachers who want note taking to be an inherent part of mathematics instruction often do these things:

- Model and guide note taking as the lesson proceeds. Use student models as well, so that other students can see that good note taking is doable.

- Have students exchange notes in mid lesson. Students can learn from each other's notes and add to their own. Also, a student who knows that a peer is going to be viewing her notes is more likely to make them presentable and comprehensible.

- Provide templates to scaffold note-taking skills.

- Include metacognition, asking students to reflect on how useful their notes turned out to be when most needed (in studying for a test or solving a problem).
- Use a student's notes as formative assessment, that is, as a diagnostic tool to match instruction with learning.
- Take a few moments at the beginning of class to have students review their notes from the day before.

Note taking is often expected, not taught; when taught, often not revisited. Let's take a moment to review some effective habits of note taking:

- Leave lots of white space on the page.
- Use color.
- Have an efficient system of abbreviation.
- Date your notes.
- Review your notes.
- Add to your notes (hence the white space!).
- Integrate the new math language (and symbols) that you are learning in your notes.
- Rework and rewrite your notes into another form. Condense your notes onto an index card. Explain your notes to your study buddy. Find pictures to go along with your notes. Anything you do to revisit and recreate your notes will solidify your learning.

Three *As* of Math Note Taking

Accuracy: Math notes obviously need to reflect accurate numbers, symbols, formulas, and formats. Students need to have and use rulers or protractors or other measurement instruments to ensure accuracy.

Appearance: Messy notes will not become a useful reference tool. This means having plenty of white space on the page, keeping columns straight, writing legible numerals and letters, avoiding confusing arrows and mind-muddling crossouts.

Application: There needs to be alignment of a student's math notes with problems that need solving. Math note taking is authentic when it is necessary to refer to the notes to do homework and classwork.

Excellent math teachers know that note-taking skills need to be incorporated into mathematics instruction, not left up to the students without any modeling or expectations.

Note Taking as a Meaning-Making Activity

In *Active Literacy Across the Curriculum* (2006, pp. 41–58), Heidi Hayes Jacobs uses the term *creative engagement* to describe effective, knowledge-building note taking as a classroom practice. It is this "interactive note taking," Jacobs says, that transforms a student from a passive receiver of information into an active learner, making meaning their own.

So how do we go from "just copying" to "creative and interactive" note taking? One way is to rethink what our students are expected to do with information. While it is true that copying a definition, the steps to a procedure, or a formula is one necessary component of mathematics class, there are other verbs to be done in the name of note taking. Students need opportunities to shape their learning by:

- Extracting
- Reacting
- Combining
- Questioning
- Predicting
- Describing
- Detailing
- Summarizing
- Paraphrasing
- Conjecturing
- Concluding
- Noticing
- Commenting

In every subject, note taking is a domain-specific competency. In English class, students should learn how to represent the key elements of a work of fiction. They should learn how to annotate a poem with commentary. They should learn how to record their own response in a dialectical journal. In social students, they should learn how to create a timeline, outline the information laid out in a textbook chapter, create a cause-and-effect chart. In science, they should learn how to record their observations as they work through a lab procedure. And for mathematics, students should learn how to record similarities and difference on a Venn diagram, create and use a matrix for feature analysis, and do other forms of categorizing using various graphic organizing formats.

Jacobs suggests four kinds of note taking:

- *Gathering and categorizing:* As students work through an authentic mathematical research project, they need to record their findings. Venn diagrams, spreadsheets, matrices, and graphs are useful structures for organizing information. Gathering and categorizing involve finding patterns of similarities and differences.

Excellent math teachers set up tasks that require students to recognize and apply mathematical concepts and principles in the world outside the classroom. Given a concept or principle, students are asked to gather examples and nonexamples. Gathering and categorizing involves list-making, and a lot of people love lists. An incomplete list serves as a "starter kit" for generating examples that follow the guiding principle of the list.

Muschla and Robert's *The Math Teacher's Book of Lists* (1995) is a well-organized compilation of more than 300 lists of encyclopedic facts about mathematics. The lists are intelligently laid out and many are supported with visuals. Here, for example is a list of Euclid's Axioms (p. 102):

- Things equal to the same thing are equal to each other.
- If equals are added to equals the sums are equal.
- If equals are subtracted from equals, the differences are equal.
- Things which coincide with one another are equal.
- The whole is greater than any of its parts.

Using gathering and categorizing as a note-taking structure, students can find examples from real life situations that illustrate the axioms.

- *Commenting and questioning:* As students figure out what's going on and what to do with a word problem, they can annotate in the margins. This gives them control of the problem: *What looks important? what looks irrelevant?*

It can help to rephrase a problem into its relevant part. When we rephrase, we can also lay the problem out on paper so that its facts are clear and separate. For example, if the problem is stated this way:

> Tess, Diana, and Erika form a garage-cleaning team to make extra money. They work together for four days, five hours each day, cleaning out and rearranging three garages in their neighborhood. They charge their clients $30 per hour. If they share the money equally, how much should each girl get?

The relevant information can be rephrased and rearranged:

- 3 girls
- 4 days, 5 hours per day = 20 hours of work
- $30 per hour × 20 hours = $600
- $600 ÷ 3 girls = $200 per girl

♦ *Organizing graphically:* A graphic organizer is a reformation of essential information into a visual display. Graphic organizers allow the viewer to take in complex information at a glance. Jacobs refers to them as "a kind of conceptual real estate" (2006, p. 51). The ability to convert sentence-and-paragraph information into a graphic organizer can establish links from mathematics into other subjects, especially science and social studies. These subjects engage in mathematical concepts (trends, patterns, maps) all the time.

Of course, mathematics is the birthplace of graphic organizers. We've always had different kinds of graphs to represent proportions, charts to represent relationships. In addition, the geometric proof, Venn diagram, truth table, tally sheet, tree diagram, even the lined-up way that basic arithmetic operations are presented on the page are all graphic organizers.

♦ *Outlining:* Outlines are about order and sequencing: *a place for everything and everything in its place*. Outlining reinforces and make visual the key concept of subordination. By looking at an outline, we can immediately answer such questions as: What belongs to what? What are some examples of a concept or a law? What are the big ideas and what smaller ideas emanate from them?

Ask a group of elementary teachers, English teachers, social studies teachers, or even science teachers what they think about incorporating outlining skills into their lessons and I'll bet you'll see some teachers trying hard to disappear. What's the problem? "It's so confusing! All those letters and numerals!" The irony is that those very people who aren't cowed by an alphanumeric system are the math teachers, and it's in math class that outlining is generally *not* seen as a useful tool!

Given the squeamishness that I have encountered among teachers when we mention outlining as a rule-governed system of note taking, I encourage math teachers to lay claim to it. It's up their alley, with its Roman numerals and linear features. I believe that the ability to transform well-organized textbook-like information is an important skill, a skill that will serve students well throughout their education. Outlining helps you concentrate, and gives you something concrete to represent the time you spent reading. The outline form is matched to the textbook form, with its headings and subheadings already pointing you to main ideas. But equally important, outlining forces you to follow directions, a very mathematical thing to do.

I think we make a mistake by throwing out the rules of outlining in favor of the looser so-called concept maps, mind maps, anything-goes formats. Those formats are appropriate for brainstorming. It is the outline form that is appropriate for recreating information that is already organized, such as that in a textbook or encyclopedia-type article. I believe that, especially in a math class, there is a definite place for adhering the rules of an outline: alternating numbers and letters; indentation; capitalization and periods; incomplete sentences (with no periods after them, for that reason); having more than a single item for each subheading. Outlining is linear, for lack of a better term, "left-brained." For our "left-brain" favoring students, it fits into the way they learn best naturally. And for our "right-brain" favoring students (I am one of these), the practice of working outside their comfort zone is much needed.

We can scaffold outlining skills as shown in Figure 6.1. We can also employ this three-step scaffolding sequence within a single school year. The idea is to have students see information in terms of larger-to-smaller relationships and then to express those relationships in increasing levels of complexity as they get used to the outline form. Another way of scaffolding is to give students outlines that are filled in at various points and have the students complete them.

Figure 6.1. Graduated Complexity of the Outline Form

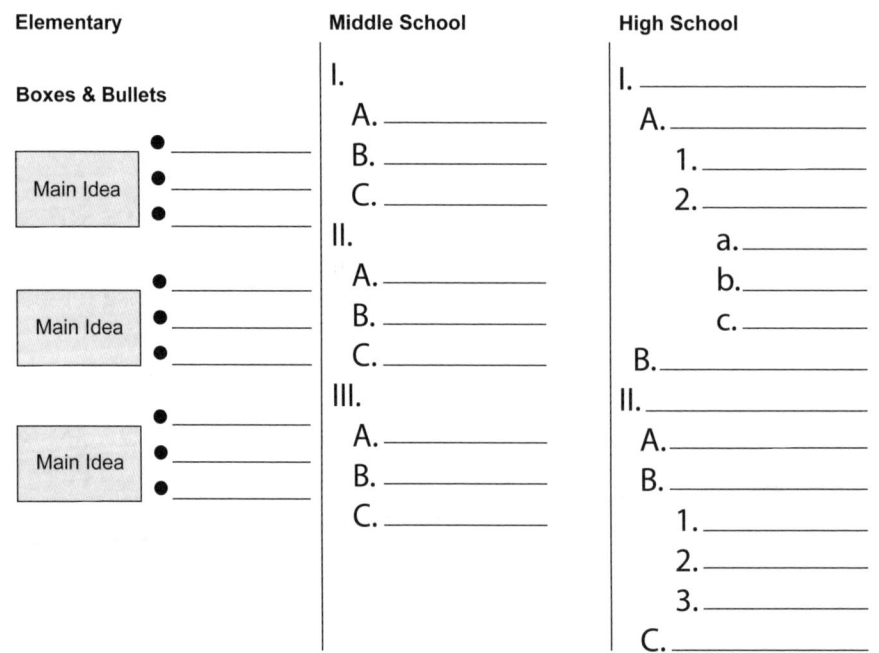

Elementary	Middle School	High School
Boxes & Bullets	I.	I. ____
	A. ____	A. ____
Main Idea — • ____	B. ____	1. ____
• ____	C. ____	2. ____
• ____	II.	a. ____
	A. ____	b. ____
Main Idea — • ____	B. ____	c. ____
• ____	C. ____	B. ____
• ____	III.	II. ____
	A. ____	A. ____
Main Idea — • ____	B. ____	B. ____
• ____	C. ____	1. ____
		2. ____
		3. ____
		C. ____

I've had teachers ask me if there is any way to make teaching outlining anything but dull. My suggestion is to animate the process, as described below by Jacobs:

> In one high school, I saw an extremely effective use of cafeteria tables to help freshmen lay out their outlines....Each student had collected many index cards with extractions on key points....The teacher asked them to put them in sets and label them with a common factor on the top. A rubber band was put around each set. She then asked the students to identify possible ways to sequence those labels, and they literally had to lay them out (like train tracks) on the cafeteria tables. When this was accomplished, the teacher had them open the banded sets and lay them under each topic. She then told them to use a Roman numeral outline system to collect the sequence of sets of topic cards and the supporting detail cards. The students got it. They understood for the first time that outlining is a superb organizer. (2006, p. 55)

Here are some topics for which the process of creating an outline can solidify meaning:

I. Kinds of...

    A. Kinds of numbers

    B. Kinds of graphs

    C. Kinds of measurements

    D. Kinds of shapes

    E Kinds of borders

    F. Kinds of groupings

    G. Kinds of fractions

II. Ways to...

    A. Ways to check your work

    B. Ways to divide (add, subtract, multiply)

    C. Ways to estimate

    D. Ways to solve for x

    E. Ways to represent fractions

III. Properties of Numbers

    A. Commutative property

  B. Associative property

  C. Distributive property

 IV. Moving a geometric figure without changing its shape

  A. Slides

  B. Flips

  C. Turns

Math and Me

 Despite my proclivity for "right-brained" (creative, nonlinear) learning and thinking, I found it easy to learn the classic Harvard outline form when I was in the fifth grade. I remember that we had to put together what would now be called a "multigenre" report about a state. Mine was Tennessee. This encyclopedic project was to be a bound collection of sentence-and-paragraph reportage on facts and figures, annotated pictures that we were expected to "send away for" by writing a formal business letter request to the proper authorities (whose addresses we were expected to locate), an outline of an encyclopedia article, and a smattering of bar graphs and pie charts. All of this was to culminate in an oral presentation replete with talking points written on index cards.

 To this day, I remember details about the state of Tennessee that have no business sticking in my head. I'll go up against any non-Tennessean in answering any question about the state (provided that the information is not dated past 1960.) Certainly, my ability to retain such facts has much to do with the multifaceted components of this massive project, not the least of which was the *outlining*.

 What that outlining allowed me to do was to take the encyclopedic information and recreate it as a skeletal form, stripped of extraneous detail. That is, of course, what an outline accomplishes. What this has to do with math learning is that I never was required to use outlining to recreate mathematical information the way I used it for social studies information. My suggestion is that outlining mathematical information would have worked just as well to help me truly *own* the concepts and supportive details.

 Actually, there *weren't any* note-taking structures or practices that were a part of my entire math education, other than copying from the board. I believe that the absence of note taking as a learning strategy left me without a way I might have had to process mathematics in a way that would have helped. One of the reasons for this book is to encourage teachers of math to model different kinds of note taking. It is the *process* of taking/making notes that constitutes the learning.

Conclusion

I'm hoping that this chapter has given you specific models for effective note taking in mathematics, and that you will view note taking as an important means for learning and owning the math. I'm hoping that, if you've been a copy-from-the-board teacher, as I was once, you will graduate from that (not abandon it completely!) into a more model-based way of teaching students to take their *own* notes.

STRATEGY 7

Using Language-Based Formative Assessment in Mathematics

Excellent teachers of mathematics use plain English to create language-based formative assessment. Formative assessment is information that students give to teachers about their learning. The purpose of formative assessment is to determine the teacher's next steps in instruction. Formative assessment affects the teacher's plan book, not her grade book.

Arguably, the most contentious issue in education as we proceed through this twenty-first century is testing: standardized testing, high-stakes testing, testing modifications for special education students, how test results should or should not affect teacher evaluation, who is accountable for what when it comes to testing, etc. But to me, the most important question involving test mania is whether or not having to be driven by a test helps or hinders *learning*. There are those who believe that testing is the perfect recipe for perfect education, that it keeps teachers focused on high standards, motivates students and rewards achievement with high grades that act as a kind of "academic paycheck." Proponents of testing believe that it keeps the stakeholders of education (i.e., everybody) properly informed about how well our students are learning. But there are those who decry testing as an artificially imposed, politically manipulated, arbitrary and unfair sham that delivers misleading and easily, sometimes deliberately misinterpreted data. The opponents of testing believe that it discourages everything from differentiated instruction to teachable moments to depth and complexity of learning. The arguments for and against testing concern *summative* assessment. Here, we will be talking about *formative* assessment, about which there can be no argument.

There can be no argument about the value of formative assessment because its *only* purpose is to give the teacher information to improve instruction for the students in front of him or her (as opposed to a group of students somewhere else in the state or nation, normed on a field tested standardized test). Formative assessment tells the teacher not only what the students do and do not know, but why they think what they think, how they go about solving a problem, where their understandings and skills are breaking down. It's the magnetic resonance imaging (MRI) of education—not just a number, but a whole picture. And that is why formative assessment in mathematics must be done through language.

In his paper to the Conference of Australian Association of Mathematics Teachers, "Keeping Learning on Track: Formative Assessment and the Regulation of Learning," Dylan Wiliam describes the key ingredients of formative assessment in mathematics: "Effective questioning, feedback, ensuring learners understand the criteria for success, and peer- and self-assessment" (n.d., p. 20).

In mathematics, Student A gets the right answer for the wrong reason. She's right on the test, but she doesn't know the math. Unless she is always this lucky, she will be wrong most of the time on this kind of question. Wiliam gives the example of a student who follows the faulty reasoning that the largest fraction is the one having the smallest denominator and the smallest fraction is the one with the largest denominator. On two items in the TIMMS exam, this student gets the right answer, even though she doesn't really understand the focus of the question, which is about how fractions work.

Here is the relevance to how language is used to ask questions:

> By asking questions of students, teachers try to establish whether students have understood what they are meant to be learning, and if students answer the questions correctly, it is tempting to assume that the students' conceptions match those of the teacher. However, all that has really been established is that the students' conceptions [happen to] fit the limitations of the questions. Unless the questions used are very rich, there will be a number of students who manage to give all the right responses, while having very different conceptions from those intended. (Wiliam, n.d., p. 21)

In other words, barebones questions leave a lot of leeway for false positives when it comes to knowing whether a student truly understands the intended concept of the question. Only "rich" questions—questions formulated by a lot of meaningful language—can determine what the student is actually thinking, and whether that thinking reflects the intended learning.

Let's say you have these simultaneous equations:

$3a = 24$

$a + b = 16$

A student I'll call James is stumped because he is operating under the assumption that a and b have to be different numbers. He was never taught this. His experience tells him that two variables, designated by different letters, have to represent different values. If the simultaneous equations were as written below, James would get the question right, but his faulty reasoning would go undetected:

$3a = 24$
$a + b = 17$

James's thinking reveals a fascinating feature of human learning: We generalize through experience. We observe rules and then apply rules, without necessarily having to have the rules explicitly pointed out to us. But in so doing, we can sometimes assume a rule—a generalization—to exist when all that existed were coincidences! It was a coincidence, not a rule, that in James's math life, two different letters always represented two different values. Scientists refer to this overgeneralization as the misattribution of correlation to a cause. (The rooster brings the dawn.)

The point, as Wiliam explains, is elegant: What students learn is not necessarily what teachers intend to teach. Formative assessment consisting of having students explain (in words) their reasoning is the antidote to having students operate on their false generalizations. Language gives us that "window into thinking" that we need to cure what ails the student who gets it right for the wrong reasons, or who, like James, is stymied because he is laboring under a false belief.

Questions and Classroom Dialogue

Here's something you see in most American mathematics classrooms: The teacher "keeps the class on its toes" by scattering lots of questions about the room. If I'm a student, I have to pay attention and not be texting my friends and updating my Facebook page lest I "get called on." The questions asked in this "scattering" model may call for the same skills to be executed by several students in a rat-a-tat fashion, or they may be based on one other in a cumulative fashion.

Some teachers employ a different way of asking questions in class. Rather than shooting the same level of questions to a variety of students (scattershot), some teachers ask a sequence of questions, each more exploratory, to a single student. Says Wiliam: "With such questions, the level of classroom dialogue can be built up to quite a sophisticated level" (n.d., p. 24). Wiliam acknowledges the difficulty of changing the game in this way: the student being asked to delve into several increasingly challenging questions may take umbrage, while the other members of the class may squirm or disengage, "but as soon as students understand that the teacher may well be asking them what they have learned from a particular exchange between another student and the teacher, their concentration is likely to be quite high" (n.d., p. 24).

Teachers need not be the only ones asking questions.

> There is substantial evidence that students' learning is enhanced by getting them to generate their own questions. If instead of writing an end-of-topic test herself, the teacher asks the students to write a test that tests the work the class has been doing, the teacher can gather useful evidence about what the students think they have been learning, which is often very different from what the teacher thinks the class has been learning. (n.d., p. 24)

Students who struggle with math tests can gain a measure of control of their anxiety when they create their own test questions. Teachers get a window into students' thoughts when they see the kinds of test questions the students produce. Student-created questions that are too easy reveal a lack of depth of understanding of what is intended to be taught, whereas questions that are far too difficult may reveal that the student is mystified and feeling defeated.

Not all solicitations of student knowledge need to be in the form of questions. A teacher can ask a simple yes/no question like "Are all squares rectangles?" Such a question is not going to take students very far in their mathematical thinking. But if the teacher presents a statement like "All squares are rectangles" and has students discuss it and present the fruits of their discussion to the class, results are going to be more interesting and informative to the teacher about what the students know and don't know.

What can be said in response to the statement "All squares are rectangles"? We might elicit conclusions that call for the use of mathematical language:

- "The size of a square does not affect the fact that it is a rectangle."
- "Not all rectangles are squares."
- "All squares and all rectangles are quadrilaterals."
- "The difference between a square and a rectangle is that all squares are equilateral but not all rectangles have equal sides."

Not that students can come up with language like this without a struggle. But it is that struggle that constitutes much richer learning of mathematics than answering a simple question.

Changing the Feedback Game: Numbers or Comments?

When teachers assess the work of students in mathematics, they are supposed to calculate the number of correct and incorrect answers and give a numerical grade, right? And the numerical grade is a percentage of one hundred, with sixty-five being the passing grade, more or less, right? And upon receiving that grade, the student gets an exact measure of how well she did, right? And there's no other way for teachers to respond to math work, right?

Why should we change that game? Could there possibly be a better way to lead students through their math journeys? In 1998, Ruth Butler conducted a study among seventh grade students in four schools in Israel. Students were given a sampling of divergent thinking tasks. At the end of the lesson, they handed in their papers and their work was assessed by a group of independent graders. One group of students received numerical grades based on correct/incorrect answers; one group was given comments such as "You thought of quite a few interesting ideas; maybe you could think of a few more" (Butler, 1998, p. 25 as cited in Wiliam). And one group was given both numerical grades and comments. After receiving this feedback, the classes went on to their next lesson, which was based on the first, the one on which they received the feedback.

The result was that the group that received the numerical grades only made no gains from the first lesson to the second. Those who did well, did well again. Those who did not do well, did not do well again. The same result was observed in the group that received both the numerical grades and the comments. But the group that received the comments alone showed a 30% improvement from the first lesson to the second.

Very interesting. It may not be surprising—it may conform with our experiences with students—that they do not improve their mathematics performance as a result of getting poor grades—that those who perform well on this Friday's test tend to perform well on next Friday's test, and the one after that. We could attribute such consistency to the "rich get richer" nature of mathematics: math success builds on cumulative skills. But we need an explanation, then, for the success of the students who received comments alone—no number grades. We also need an explanation for why there was no improvement when both numerical grades and commentary were given. It's as if the commentary—however tactful and accurate it may have been—didn't stand a chance against the negative feedback of the numerical grade.

Apparently, commentary alone is helpful feedback, helpful in that it results in improved performance. But when the commentary consists only of praise, as demonstrated by another Ruth Butler study, the students do not fare as well as when the commentary consists of praise for that which is praiseworthy, but also encouragement, suggestions, observations, redirections, reminders. Most of all, the comments are helpful when they are about things that the student feels are within his or her control. If Janie gets comments about a topic that is over and done with, she is not going to benefit. She will benefit if she has another bite at the apple, now that she knows how to be a better biter.

The North Carolina Department of Public Instruction (2003) says this about formative assessment in mathematics class:

> Assessment has taken on a broader meaning. Beyond grading students, assessment should probe beneath right answers to discover how students think and how instruction can be improved. In this view of assessment, expected outcomes are set and the time necessary for each student to achieve the intended outcomes varies.

In other words, if not everyone is expected to perform at the same pace, then not everyone can be expected to take the same tests at the same time. This is a radical departure from the way most classes, schools, and state education departments function. But if everyone has to take the same tests at the same time, what is the point of gathering information about student learning that would necessitate differentiation?

Do the math. If formative assessment gives information that student—we'll call her Emma—is not understanding a current topic, upon which future topics depend, and we are tied to a given test on a given date, then we can:

- Do nothing.
- Provide remediation.
- Change the content of the test for Emma.
- Change the date of the test for Emma.

If we operate within a system where the content and date of the test are not negotiable, that leaves us with the options of doing nothing (and I think we know how that's going to play out) and providing remediation. That is what Response to Intervention is all about, but Emma has to be part of her own remediation. She needs to practice to get better at math, and her homework may not look the same as that of the other students while she is in catch-up mode. And, yes, that does mean employing other modes of instruction that may have to be more language-based than traditional mathematics instruction.

How Teachers Can Use Language Modes to Assess Learning

Formative assessment in mathematics is not just numbers, symbols, and shapes. We need to know how students think and we know that through their language—speaking and writing. "Class discussion" alone is insufficient because the typical class discussion is not at discussion at all but a Q&A

volley between the teacher and a handful, if that, of the best students in the class.

That is why teachers need more verbal and written feedback from more students. Cooperative learning, math journals, annotated show-your-work displays, and individual conferences are helpful formative assessments. By listening to student conversations and reading student explanations and processes, we can know:

- What strategies are being used? Are they effective?
- What assumptions are the students making? Are they accurate?
- What do the students do when their first strategy does not work?
- How effective are the student's communication skills in mathematics? Does the student use accurate math vocabulary? Is their language specific? Do others understand them?
- In cooperative learning situations, is the student focused on the problem, as opposed to being distracted, disengaged, passive?

Teachers who rely entirely on their own voices or on quiet classrooms cannot get this information about students. Without hearing or reading the student's language, they cannot remediate, they can only repeat instruction that did not hit the mark in the first place.

Below is a list of writing-in-math task verbs that generate useful information about what students understand in mathematics:

- Observe and describe something.
- Explain how to do a procedure.
- Create a word web.
- Write a paragraph that uses a given list of terms.
- Express numbers in words.
- Write a story that uses mathematics.
- Write an acrostic about a math term.
- Observe and report about something.
- Explain what something is.
- Show that you understand something.
- Compare two things.
- Explain what you don't understand and what it is about it that confuses you.

- Write a haiku (7 syllables/ 5 syllables/ 7 syllables) about a math word or process.
- Make a crossword puzzle about math.
- List something.
- Justify an answer.
- Compose your own word problems.
- Translate a diagram, graph, or chart into words.
- Annotate a "show your work."
- Change the lyrics to a song to make it about math.
- Find patterns, name and describe them.

Conclusion

I'm hoping that this chapter has given you a clear idea of what formative assessment is and how it applies to mathematics. Numbers are not the only kind of feedback for informing students of their progress in mathematics. In fact, quantitative metrics are arguably the least effective form of feedback. Commentary without numbers has been shown to result in better student outcomes. Language activities—speaking and writing—are used by teachers to understand student learning trends and to direct instruction accordingly.

STRATEGY 8

Connecting Memorization to Meaning in Mathematics

Excellent teachers of mathematics use plain English to have students transcend memorization, connecting memorized information to meaning. There will always be controversy about the value of memorization. On one side are those who take for granted that mathematics facts (multiplication tables, single-digit addition and subtraction facts), definitions, and formulas must be memorized. On the other side are the constructivists, who reject rote memorization in favor of discovery learning, which they claim is more durable. In this chapter, I propose a blended approach, where the teachers help the students use language to connect meaning to memorized information.

Math, Mental Math, and Memorization

Let's examine the role that memorization plays in understanding, remembering, and being able to apply and manipulate the facts of mathematics. We hear a good deal of lamenting about the lack of memorization that contemporary students are taught. There are those who appear to believe that if only we would return to that Golden Age of Memorization, all our educational and societal problems would be solved.

And we hear from educators that "rote memorization" is right up there with "teaching to the test" and "look it up in the dictionary and use it in a sentence" as an outdated teaching practice. Deservedly so. By "rote memorization," we mean memorization of information, almost always in a particular order, without any connection to meaning or reason, without a governing principle, without reflection. For example, an American student should know what the fifty states of America are. She can memorize them alphabetically. But it would be far more meaningful, memorable, and useful to learn them by connecting them to a geographical principal or historical principal: The states of the Northeast, the Midwest, the Far West, etc. It would be even better to break the regions down further: The states of the Great Pacific North-west, the Deep South, the Plains, etc. It would also make sense to group the states under a historical principle: the thirteen original colonies, the states that were part of Mexico, the states included in the Louisiana Purchase. Who would ever attempt to teach children the fifty states by memorization alone: no *map, no jigsaw puzzle, no stories*! Students who used memorization alone, with no organizing principle other than alphabetical order (which is irrelevant to meaning) are missing great opportunities to understand something about geography and history, information that is not only intrinsically valuable, but that embeds the memorized information and increases the likelihood of retrieval.

The truth is that memorization without understanding—memorization that is disconnected from meaning—is not good education. Memorization without understanding of reasons, without recognition of patterns, without sense-making connections, is not useful and is easily forgettable. Search your own memory. If you are like me, you have shards of memorized maxims that mean absolutely nothing to you: For example, my mind has retained the mnemonic "Please Excuse My Dear Aunt Sally," but, I have long, long ago forgotten what it means and how I used it. It isn't that mnemonics are bad to have; it's that mnemonics are useful only to the extent that what they stand for is connected to meaning.

Memorizing Tables and Sequences

When I was in the fourth grade, I had trouble with my multiplication tables. I could do the one-times and two-times, the five-times, and all the "twins" (six times six; eight times eight, etc.). I could do the nines by adding zero to the number and subtracting one. I could do the elevens. I could do the eights the way I did the nines, but subtracting two. But when it came to all the others, I'd have to mentally recite the tables, and I wasn't always right. When I got up past forty, the numbers got mixed up in my head. Forty-two, forty-eight, and fifty-four were especially "hard." I couldn't seem to find a pattern to distinguish them.

The thing is, I thought the way I knew the multiplication combinations that I did know was "the wrong way to learn," a kind of "cheating." Thinking, as I did, that memorization and immediate production of the right answer was the proper way to learn multiplication, I tried to train my mind to do that, rather than to "figure out" the answer by anchoring it into the patterns that I knew, such as the five pattern. Back in those days (the period of history before the calculator but after the abacus), speed in multiplication was highly valued. Hence, flash cards.

The teacher would mix up the flash cards and put them in front of your face. In a nanosecond, you were required to produce the product of the two numbers shown. My classmates could do this; I could not. That inability necessitated my reporting to school extra early for private drill sessions with my fourth grade teacher, Mrs. Josephson. Those extra help sessions were duly fortified by my parents, who were also armed with flashcards.

I liked Mrs. Josephson, though I don't know if I appreciated her getting to her job early to work just with me. But I didn't want to disappoint her, or embarrass myself before the school day even started. I did my best. I bounced the answers back like a champion ping-pong player. What Mrs. Josephson didn't know was that, as she sat with her back to the windows, the morning sunlight shone in through the flash cards, making them translucent enough for me to see the answers through them. I even pretended to be stumped every few cards, so not to set off alarms. That is how I got through the fourth grade.

Although my way may was about two seconds slower than the rote memorization of the tables, my way made more sense and revealed a pattern. Had Mrs. Josephson asked me what I knew, rather than drill me on what I did not know, had she helped me expand my system, had she combined the memorization with the meaning making, I wouldn't have had to rely on sunlight to beam through the flash cards to do multiplication.

There's no doubt that many educators and lay people value memorization and recitation of the multiplication table. If we think of mathematics being about recitation and calculation alone, then we might believe strongly in the value of memorizing alone. Indeed, many of our assessments do not call for more than calculation and execution of algorithms. But if we think of mathematics as a system of relationships and patterns that can be understood and even admired, as developing the mental equipment to solve problems, then we see the limits of memorization. Memorizing the multiplication table does not necessarily illuminate the relationship between multiplication and addition.

What does this discussion have to do with our theme of the language-rich classroom? Well, it's language that makes the multiplication tables something more than mindless recitation. My experience with Mrs. Josephson was the perfect example of what mathematics looks like without language! She and I and the flashcards were devoid of language, and *I couldn't learn very well without language!* With enough drill, I could perform on cue, but it would have taken language to explain the relationships within the cells on the multiplication table to get me to understand what multiplication was really all about.

We value memorization/recitation of the multiplication table because we value speed. The child who has memorized multiplication facts can produce answers instantly. A child like the one that I once was needs to think for a second or two about relationships. I acknowledge that many students of this and previous generations have gotten along fine by memorizing the multiplication tables and responding to flash cards. My objection is having memorization be the *only* method of teaching multiplication, with speed being, in my opinion, overly valued.

And now it's time for the "baby and the bathwater" disclaimer: I am not advocating for the banishment of multiplication tables or the ability to memorize and recite them. I am advocating for differentiation, and for using language to mediate between conceptual understanding and recitation.

Memorizing Definitions vs. Knowing What Something Is

Mathematics class is full of definitions. But if you look at the definitions found in a math textbook glossary through the eyes of a learner, not an expert, you'll discover problems: The student who can recite that the "least common denominator" is "the least common multiple of the denominators of two or more factors" (Math to Know, p. 454) may not know how to find the least common denominator for a set of fractions, may not be able to recognize an least common denominator, may not be able to manipulate one. Unless the words in the definition translate from an abstract concept into a concrete image, the memorized definition is not helpful.

Most of the words (and phrases) we know have not been learned because someone gave us a definition. Most of the words we know come to us through the three *Ex*s: *experience, exposure, examples*. We've figured words (and phrases) out for ourselves as a result of having them attached to familiar experiences. The words have been repeated in a meaningful context that bonds the word to the concept. And we have come to know the words based on their embodiments: examples. Nothing is more powerful than examples to teach the meaning of a word.

The definitions do need to be memorized, but how do we know that the concepts are understood, that the scripted language has real meaning? Linguists talk about language in terms of *register*. The register is the "attitude" of the language—it may be formal, conversational, slang, technical, etc. When chunks of language are memorized and recited verbatim, such as the safety speech that flight attendants make at the beginning of the flight, we call that *frozen register*, also called scripted language. Scripted language is comfortable, but, like all language, if the user doesn't understand it, it's useless. The problem is that mathematical language as expressed in definitions has to be precise. What the definition is seeking to do is to carve out specific territory that is limited only to the world of mathematics. Any deviations are likely to contaminate the definition with nonmathematical applications.

Word learning is a recursive and layered process. That is why a toddler may designate orange juice, coffee, and soda pop with the same inaccurate noun *milk*. Only through depth of experience does the toddler learn to differentiate beverages by their various attributes and eventually call each by its specialized name. On the way, the toddler is applying known term, *milk*, too broadly, yes, but not illogically.

Word learning is dynamic. Our understanding of words like *property, value, evaluate, common, point, function, order* narrows to fit specific mathematical contexts. The teacher who demands that students cut off their knowledge of such terms in the vernacular from how they are used in the world of mathematics is misguided. She may think that "it would be too confusing" to mix vernacular knowledge of a term with its mathematical meaning, but known information helps shape new information. Besides, the mind can't help making associations as it tries to integrate new understandings.

In her report that appeared in *The Mathematics Educator*, high school mathematics teacher Revathy Parameswaran (2010) talks about the stages of understanding mathematical definitions. The first stage is getting familiar with the language of the formalized written definition, including the symbols that denote it on paper. In the second stage, the learner develops a mental model ("semantic cloud") that represents the concept denoted by its definition. It is important to note that the mental model transcends the words in the definition alone: words in a recited or recognized definition do not automatically and immediately create an image. The third stage is the ability to generate several examples. And the fourth stage is the ability to the concept in its mathematical context: How is it used in theorems? So, while the first two stages are static (the definition comes to exist in the mind of the learner), the third and fourth stages are dynamic (the definition enters a context).

According to Parameswaran, the instructional implications of the way in which mathematical definitions are learned incrementally, as described above, are that:

- Teachers need to understand how definitions develop in the student's mind in stages. An unripe definition cannot be applied to problem solving.

- Teachers can move the process along by offering an array of examples. Examples bring a newly learned definition into the student's schema (cognitive framework).

- Teachers can help students understand that a definition, like a tangible object, may be used for multiple and creative purposes.

- When students use their definitions repeatedly to solve problems, their understandings of the definitions are continuously sharpened.

Conclusion

That which is memorized is rigid and forgettable, whereas that which is *understood* is flexible and durable. When we are tempted to have students memorize something—a definition, a table, a formula—we should find a way to couple the memorization with an understanding of the concept, the pattern, the rationale.

STRATEGY 9

Incorporating Writing-to-Learn Activities in Mathematics

Excellent teachers of mathematics use plain English to incorporate writing both as a means for learning and in assessments. Writing does more than express what we already know: Writing causes learning. By writing, we create, transform, mobilize, integrate, and secure what might otherwise be fragile knowledge. Writing whips learning into shape!

By "fragile knowledge," I mean knowledge that will soon be forgotten. The human brain does its best to be an efficient machine. When information in it goes unused, it simply discards that information in a process that scientists call *neurological pruning*, or *synaptic pruning*, or *neurostructural reassembling*. We nonscientists call this process *forgetting*, or the *use-it-or-lose it* principle. The act of writing—whether that be in snippets such as an annotation of a solution, a list, class notes, or fully developed sentences, paragraphs, and reports—helps us retain information. Writing in mathematics is a pervasive strategy, which is why we've already talked about note taking, creation of original word problems, and formative assessment. In this chapter, we will go into further detail about writing-to-learn strategies.

What Kinds of Writing Work Best for Mathematics Learners?

Not all writing is beneficial to learning. Many students simply will not write outside of school, and requiring them do so—however beneficial it might have been for them had they done it—results in, so to speak, a whole 'nother thing. Teachers get worn down by the pushback from students, parents, and sometimes administrators dismayed at the quarterly grades shot by the bullets in the no-homework gun. If we are to have students do their writing in class, how do we know that they are learning as much as they would have if they were experiencing other instruction?

We are never more than one click away from finding a reputable and recent study that affirms the value of writing to learn, remember, and use *any* set of facts, including mathematics. But what kinds of writing, and for what purposes, and for what audiences, is writing most beneficial for mathematics learning? A study done at the National Research Center for English Learning and Achievement by Bangert-Drowns, Hurley, and Wilkenson (2007) concludes as follows:

> In three-fourths of the studies, writers outperformed conventional students but the typical improvement was a small one. In twenty-four of the forty-five studies, students completed writing assignments in class, so researchers could record time spent on writing tasks. What appears to matter more than the amount of time given to the assignment is the nature of the writing task, the kind of thinking that gets done. One factor reliably enhanced the effect of writing-to-learn. When writing prompts urged students to reflect on their writing process—the challenges they faced and the strategies they employed—the educative effects of writing were substantially improved.
>
> In general, these studies and other research suggest that writing can benefit learning, not so much because it allows personal expression about subject matter as because it scaffolds metacognitive reflection on the learning process....Even relatively brief tasks can boost learning. (para. 5–6)

To summarize, the kind of writing that is most helpful for mathematics is the kind that gets them to look inward at their own learning styles, pacing, processes, obstacles, and successes. The simple graphic organizer shown in Figure 9.1 can be used to help students on a daily or weekly basis to put their learning into words. This structure is particularly useful for special education students.

Reasons for *Not* Including Writing in Mathematics

Teachers of mathematics give several reasons for not including writing in math class. I will address three of them:

- ♦ Lack of skill in teaching and responding to student writing
- ♦ Lack of class time to devote to writing
- ♦ Strong beliefs about traditional teaching methods

Figure 9.1. Self-Reflection Graphic Organizer

My Progress Report

What I understand today:

What I don't understand yet:

What I need:

Lack of Skill in Teaching and Responding to Student Writing

Teaching writing is far from simple. Teachers who are trained as generalists for elementary grades usually feel more comfortable than those trained to teach mathematics exclusively. But all teachers can include writing in math lessons if they start slowly and build on their skills. Start with lists, annotations of solutions, and graphic organizers. Then move into one-or-two-sentence responses.

What can you expect? If you are not accustomed to reading student writing, prepare to read many, many errors. Writing is a sophisticated skill that is learned incrementally over many years. That is why students take English Language Arts classes every year of their K–12 education, and that is why they take Composition 101 in college. Expect students to "write the way they speak." Conventions of written English, like spelling, capitalization, punctuation, and paragraphing, are not applicable to spoken language, and many students take a very long time to transition from speech to writing. That leaves you in a quandary about how to respond to speech-like writing without turning mathematics class into English class. Stick to a few clear guidelines:

- Insist on reasonable neatness and legibility.

- Require reasonable attention to spelling, capitalization, and punctuation.
- Have a policy about rejecting written work that demonstrates substandard effort.
- Use a simple rubric that scores for factual accuracy, organization, use of math terminology, and overall presentation.

If you score with a rubric, such as that shown in Figure 9.2, students will see what they are being held accountable for, their strengths and weaknesses, and their progress.

Figure 9.2. Math Writing Rubric

	4 points	3 points	2 points	1 points
Information	Lots of detailed, accurate information	Some detailed, accurate information	One or two examples of detailed, accurate information	No detailed, accurate information
Language	Lots of math terms	Some math terms	One or two math terms	No math terms
Presentation	Easy to read, very neat, care taken in spelling, capitalization, punctuation	Easy to read, fairly neat, a few errors in spelling, capitalization, punctuation	A little hard to read, could be neater, several errors in spelling, capitalization, punctuation	Hard to read, does not show respect for the reader's time, needs to be proofread

Lack of Class Time to Devote to Student Writing

Begin or end class with five minutes of writing. If writing-to-learn activities fulfill their promise, you will find that a few minutes several times a week pays for itself in improved student performance as well as formative assessment. Rather than playing Q&A with the few confident students whose hands are always up, try giving the whole class one minute to compose a response, share it with a partner, and then with the class. This is called a think-pair-share activity.

Strong Beliefs About Traditional Mathematics Instruction

Including writing in mathematics is something of a paradigm shift, but hardly new or risky. In traditional mathematics instruction, communication between teacher and students is limited to assessment on right-or-wrong tests and classroom Q&A. Given what we know about the importance of formative assessment and differentiation, those two forms of feedback can hardly be considered sufficient.

Short Writing Assignments: A Model

Joann Bossenbroek (n.d.) of Columbus State Community College describes how short writing assignments help students clarify concepts and provide formative assessments to drive instruction. Her assessment technique, she says, "helps students learn how to use mathematical language precisely. It helps me check whether they have absorbed the distinctions that language is trying to establish and the details of the principal concepts" (para. 1).

Her method is to hand out several questions before each test. The questions require students to use correct mathematical terminology to explain, describe, compare, contrast, or define given concepts that will be on the test in some way. Bossenbroek's questions are carefully crafted and have multiple parts:

> [Example (Intermediate Algebra)]: In your own words, *define* "function." *Give an example* of a relationship that is a function and one that is not and *explain* the difference.

Bossenbroek writes that her students admit that these writing assignments "force them to think" rather than just "work the problems."

> These assignments have helped me improve my teaching. They have given me a better understanding of what it is about a specific concept that is confusing. Then I carefully tailor my examples in class to address the ambiguities.

We can scale this questioning model to make it appropriate for pre-Algebra:

Example 1: Explain what it means to factor a number. Compare factoring to prime factorization. Give an example of each.

Example 2: Define prime number. Give an example and a nonexample and explain why the nonexample is not a prime number.

Example 3: Explain the difference between the least common multiple and the least common denominator.

Example 4: Explain the process of adding fractions by using the least common denominator.

Example 5: Define unlike fractions and give an example and a nonexample.

Four Types of Writing-to-Learn Mathematics

In *Mathematics the Write Way: Activities for Every Elementary Classroom* (1996), Marilyn S. Neil suggests expository, expressive, creative, and processed writing.

The purpose of *expository* writing is to explain or describe content. Expository writing for mathematics can take the form of complete sentences and paragraphs or lists and annotations.

Perhaps the most convenient prompt for expository writing in mathematics is to ask students to describe the process of solving a problem. This can be done in a journal, with a first person account: "How I solved the problem." Or, it can be done as a procedural report, as instructions: "How to solve the problem."

Expository writing can also explain information that is in graphic form. Students can be asked to peruse the newspaper or the Internet for information presented in graphic form and then explain in words what the graph means. By recreating graphic information in verbal form, students reinforce their knowledge of graphs.

The prompts *explain, describe, analyze, compare,* and *summarize* lead to expository writing. If you want the writing to be metacognitive, ask for a first person response:

- Explain how you…
- Explain why you…
- Describe how you…
- Describe what you did to solve…
- Analyze the steps you took to…

- Compare how you solved…to how you solved…
- Summarize what you've learned about…

The second form of writing that Marilyn Neil delineates is *expressive* writing. This is the type of writing in which students "express and document their mathematical thoughts," or to think on paper. Expressive writing is informal, individualistic, and spontaneous. It is the kind of writing that students do in journals. The audience can be the teacher and other students, who should be expected to respond in writing. The value of expressive writing is that it allows students to work through anxieties about mathematics and to acknowledge their progress. Expressive writing is often accompanied by pictures and drawings. The journal is also a great place for students to include actual mathematical structures, such as Venn diagrams, graphs, matrices, tables, continuums, and charts to express their feelings and progress, background knowledge, and degrees of understanding about what they are learning in mathematics.

Creative writing, although done mostly in connection with language arts, is another form of writing that can strengthen learning in mathematics. Creative writing appropriate for mathematics can include poetry, stories, and skits. Poetry, because it has a meter, already has a mathematical component. Here, we'll talk about two forms of poetry: the haiku and the cinquain.

The Japanese-inspired haiku is a nonrhyming little wisp of language consisting of three lines, seventeen syllables, in the pattern of 5–7–5. Authentic haiku capture an image from nature, but, in this case, we'll capture a concept in mathematics. We can use a math term as our title and then describe it in our haiku, or we can include the math term within the haiku. We can use the math term literally or metaphorically.

Haiku that uses the math term as the title:

Perimeter

Polygons have sides

This goes around the edges:

The sum of the lengths

Remainder

After division

It's the number left over

That doesn't fit in

A cinquain is a five-line, nonrhyming poem whose lines fall into this pattern:

Line 1: two syllables (noun)

Line 2: four syllables (two adjectives describing the noun)

Line 3: six syllables (three verbs giving the actions of the noun)
Line 4: eight syllables (a complete sentence)
Line 5: two syllables (repetition of the noun, or a synonym)

An example of a math cinquain is:

Fractions
Partial, portion
Splitting, breaking, sharing
They're components of the whole thing
Pieces

The possibilities for embedding mathematical words and concepts in creative writing are too numerous to mention, but here are a few more ideas that students can enjoy while reinforcing their knowledge of mathematics:

- Mini-mysteries, where the solution is dependent on recognizing a mathematical falsehood;

- Traditional stories and fairy tales, where a mathematics problem is inserted as part of the story;

- Parodies of song lyrics, where math words and concepts replace some of the words;

- Advice columns, where the advice sought is about mathematics; and,

- Mixes and matches in which you present a list of nouns and prepositional phrases and ask students to combine them in a way that starts, finishes, or is in the middle of a story. But the story also has to have some kind of math problem in it. For example: *in the car, a tuxedo, an all-you-can-eat buffet, a valuable gem, a treasure chest, behind the barn, a lost cat.*

Conclusion

I'm hoping that after reading this chapter you have lots of ideas about why and how to use writing to help students learn mathematics. Admittedly, having students write is a big commitment of class time and teacher time outside of class to plan and respond to student writing. I hope that, if you try including writing as part of a language-rich mathematics class, you keep it simple and manageable.

STRATEGY 10

Preparing Students for Algebraic Thinking

Excellent teachers of mathematics use plain English to prepare students for algebraic thinking. Beginning in the elementary grades, even the primary grades, students should learn the rudiments of algebraic thinking. *A student's success in Algebra I has been found to be a predictor of whether that student will graduate from high school!* According to a report by Rutgers University (2007),

> The highest level completed math course is a strong predictor of graduation [from college]: students stopping with Algebra I have an 8 percent chance of graduating; Geometry 23 percent; Algebra II 40 percent; Trigonometry 62 percent; Pre-Calculus 74 percent; and Calculus 80 percent. A student taking a single remedial course is six times less likely to graduate. ("America's Perfect Storm," p. 3)

The Common Core State Standards do provide for a smooth transition from arithmetic to algebra by introducing algebraic concepts, in an age-appropriate manner, in the primary grades. The authors of the Common Core State Standards for mathematics aligned the standards with those used in Japan so that by grade four students are expected, in both the United States and Japan, to be "fluent at adding, subtracting, and multiplying with whole numbers; understand and be able to apply place value; and be able to classify simple two-dimensional geometric figures. These expectations form the basis for basic mathematical understanding in elementary school" (Achieve, August 2010).

Because of the emphasis on algebra in the middle grades, students need a strong lead-up to its concepts and language long before then.

Algebra is hard—and teaching algebra is hard—for four reasons, as I see it:

- *Abstractions:* Algebra lives in a world of abstractions. While the idea of using letters to substitute for numbers may seem clear to you, it is a new idea to students, and not a simple one to grasp.

- *Vocabulary:* Algebra uses unfamiliar-sounding, multisyllabic words that have to be understood in the precise context of algebra. Many of the definitions of algebraic words and terms include language that is as unfamiliar as the word or term being defined. The word "algebra" itself is new and, being of Arabic and not Latin origin, unrelated to other words in most students' vocabulary.

- *Background knowledge:* Algebra assumes fluency in the basic operations and understandings of arithmetic. Even having that, algebra gallops along, continuing to assume understandings that build on each other.

- *Strangeness:* This is an encapsulation of the above three difficulties. The student who is hit with algebra for the first time in the middle grades wonders what it is, how it got here, whatever in the world it is good for, and when it will go away. It's hard to see the real world application of algebra on one's own. It appears to complicate what should be simple. It uses a variety of new symbols. Parents are not always supportive or helpful when it comes to their children learning algebra: "This is where I can't help you anymore," "I don't remember this stuff," and, of course, "Your mother and I were never any good at math either. You come by it [your difficulties] naturally. Don't worry about it. You'll turn out fine."

Remember, I speak from the experience of one who was mystified by algebra in the seventh grade—a still-stinging memory. That is why I applaud efforts to introduce algebraic thinking in the elementary and primary grades, scaffolding both the concepts and the language.

Linking Algebra to Grammar

Grammar is like algebra in many ways. Both are "slot-and-filler" systems. That is, a sentence, like an equation, has slots (subjects, predicates, objects, complements, etc.) and those slots are filled with variables (words and phrases that will make sense in relation to other words in the other slots of the sentence).

You can prepare elementary students for algebraic thinking by teaching grammar *alongside* math. Your explanation can sound like this:

English sentences can have as few as two slots: Subject and predicate:

   Birds fly.
   Bees sting.
   Dogs bark.

Ask students to get the feel of this simple pattern by choosing any subject and generating 10 sentences about it.

   Pattern: Subject + Predicate.

You can have students write their subjects on one index card, predicate on another. Then, have them mix and match the subjects and the predicates. If they've followed the pattern (mathematical thinking), all combinations will yield sentences that are grammatically possible, if not realistically possible or probable.

Example: Jesse chooses the topic of sports to write his 10 sentences. He has:

   Goalies guard.
   Goalies defend.
   Pitchers pitch.
   Batters bat.
   Referees decide.
   Golfers swing.
   Skaters skate.
   Runners run.
   Runners steal.
   Scorekeepers tally.

The next step is to ask Jesse to notice a pattern that all of these sentences fall into. He notices that there are only two words in each sentence, that the first word does some kind of action, that the action is named in the second word. He notices that all of the "first word" words are plural, most of them having an *–ers* ending. He notices that in many cases, the second word in the pattern consists of the root of the first word. All of these observations are mathematical observations taking place in the *context* of language. Next, we help Jesse draw a framework for these sentences. That framework would consist of a rudimentary sentence diagram:

   _____   _____ .

If we call the first slot *X* and we call the second slot *Y*, we see that we can insert any number of English words into either of the slots. And we see that

> $X + Y = S$ (for sentence). It is at this point that we can introduce the term variable. If the students already know the terms *subject* and *predicate*, we can explain that subjects and predicates can be filled by various words, and that is why we call the set of those words that can fill the subject and predicate slot *variables*. In sentence making, our variables are words; in math our variables are numbers. In both cases, we can temporarily fill the slots with X and Y until we decide what the words and numbers are going to be in this particular sentence.

If this grammar-math connection works for you and your students, you can go on to draw parallels between the sentence formula (grammatical slots) and an algebraic formula. The parallel is based on a simple concept: There is a pattern. The pattern can be closed (numbers and/or words) are already filled in; or the pattern can be open (one or more numbers or words are ready to be filled in). When filled in (closed), the pattern has to make sense. It will make sense based on the other slots of the pattern.

Linking Algebra to a Lesson in Nutrition

A balanced meal, as elementary students should know, has certain food groups. There are plates called "compartment plates" that toddlers eat from (although I'm not sure why, since toddlers are not well known for either keeping things in designated compartments or caring a lot about food groups at a given meal). Those compartments are to be filled by variables. If one compartment already contains chicken, and another already contains a vegetable, we would expect that third compartment to be filled by some kind of starch (rice, potatoes, pasta, etc.).

Linking Algebra to a Workout at the Gym

Gym rats know that a good hour-long workout consists of various elements: a ten-to-fifteen-minute cardio warmup followed by ten minutes of squats, balance and lunging, followed by a few sets of upper and then lower body, and some ab work. It's a formula.

At the gym, we have all kinds of equipment for each of the elements of a workout. Hence, the workout can be represented by an algebraic equation, with the variables being the exercises and machines for each area of the body being worked on.

Conclusion

Clearly, the possibilities for algebraic thinking apply to any slot-and-filler system. If you can combine the concept of variables with something other than numbers, you can create a link that will make sense to elementary students. That link, that building of familiarity with the concept and language of variables, can be greatly helpful to students when they learn more about algebra later on. Considering the relationship between achievement in algebra and the likelihood of college graduation, it becomes extremely important to scaffold algebraic thinking as early as possible. (The Common Core State Standards do call for the teaching of basic algebraic thinking in the primary grades.)

APPENDIX 1

Word Components Commonly Seen in Math Language: Or... Words Have Cousins?

You know about word components that denote specific numbers (*uni, bi, tri, quart, pent*, etc.). The word components listed here are those that you might not already include in your teaching. And, if you do include them, perhaps you would like to extend your instruction to include the various examples that may reach outside of the math world to make connections to other fields of knowledge.

Why include information about word components in a math class? Simply because doing so creates a deeper understanding of the words. Not long ago I was in front of a ninth grade English Language Arts class doing a vocabulary lesson. The word I was teaching happened to be *soliloquy*, a monologue spoken by a character all alone on the stage. I explained to the students that soliloquy is a cousin of the words *solo* and *dialogue* and *monologue*. One student was clearly not buying it: "Words have cousins?" he asked, not without a hint of snarky suspicion.

"Yes," I informed him. "Words have cousins. They have brothers and sisters, aunts and uncles, grandparents, children, and friends. Words are related to other words. Just like people, words in the same family usually look something alike." After I pointed out the visual similarity between *soliloquy* and *solo*, and how both had to do with a performance by a single person, my student, ever the skeptic, pointed out that *monologue* and *dialogue* look nothing like *soliloquy*. He was right in one way, wrong in another. I explained that, in fact, the way the English language has evolved, the *gue* of *dialogue* and *monologue* (also *prologue, epilogue*) sometimes morphs into *qui* (as in *soliloquy, colloquial*). Not only that, but the root *–logue* means *thought*, and we see its relatives in the words *logic, apology*, and all the famous *–ology* words!

In making this explanation and giving the examples, I was broadening the students' understanding of how language works, demystifying it, and giving them tools to break down new words, especially long ones. Although I threw some words at them that I didn't expect them to already know or remember, I was sowing the seeds of background knowledge so that when the time comes to learn words like *colloquial* and *epilogue*, they will have had at least one exposure to the sounds of them. This is how language is acquired.

The best way to use a list like this is to consider the words now buzzing in your math class. Look at the prefix or combining forms that apply to these words and see if you get any ideas about linking your math words to other math words and to words in the wider language that your students already know, plus some that they need to know. Gradually, you will build up your repertoire of word knowledge, and your math lessons will become more interesting, your students' learning more durable.

I've used the term *prefix* loosely to mean a morpheme (letter combination that has a meaning) that appears at the beginning of a word. I've used the term *combining form* or *root* to refer to a morpheme that appears either at the beginning of a word or in the middle. Generally, roots appear in the middle of a word, while combining forms may appear at the beginning or in the middle.

You'll see that word components are chameleons. Along the highways and byways of language, similar-sounding letters morph from one to the other, the most common being C and G. Thus, the words *contact* and *integer* emanate from the same root. Understanding the ambiguities of how words are related calls for flexibility, itself an important habit of mind to cultivate. When we think of math as being only about "right and wrong answers," we are not being flexible. Arguably, mental flexibility and tolerance for ambiguity are faculties that are often disengaged in math class. When we closely examine word families to discern relationships among them, we are actually doing the very mathematical activity of pattern finding.

Most of these word components derive from the Indo-European ancestor of Latin and Greek, later to develop into French and, later than that, English. It is through Indo-European ancestry that we link our language to Sanskrit and other Eastern tongues. Over the years and miles, the sounds and spellings change, sometimes beyond easy recognition. But to the trained linguistic eye, the connections are discernible. I've listed only the most obvious ones, but know that etymology is an endlessly fascinating pursuit, yielding amazing insights into the *what* and the *why* of distantly related words.

The Prefixes

- ad: *ad*, often appearing as *a-*, denotes proximity. We can explain it to students as meaning "to, at, near." The most obvious example from the math world is the word *add*, along with its relatives (*addition, addend, additive*). The words *adjacent, adjoin,* and *aggregate* also fall into this group. The surprising connection is that the *ad-* prefix often masquerades as *a* in other words beginning with *a-* and having something to do with proximity: *approximate, associate, appreciate, assume, attract, admit.*

- **ambi**: Most students know the word *ambidextrous*, probably because it represents an interesting and personal concept. People are generally very definite about their lateral preferences, their *handedness*. For most of us, ambidexterity is a fascinating and strange talent. So, *ambidextrous* is a great starting point for teaching this word component. Related words are *ambivalent, amphibian, ambiguous, unambiguous, disambiguate,* and *amphitheater*. The root *ambi*, sometimes seen as *amphi*, actually means *around*, though it is often thought to mean *both*.

- **ang**: Not surprisingly, this prefix denotes *angle*. Students already know what an angle is. They know the word triangle, and probably already think of it as being comprised of the components *tri* and *angle* (three angles). It's a short hop to *quadrangle, rectangle, angular*. They may need to make the explicit connection to the derivatives of these words, such as: *triangulate, triangulation, angularity, birectangular, equiangular, pentangle*.

- **ant**: Denoting the concept of *front* or *forward*, we see this prefix most directly in the phrase *anterior angles* and in the word *antecedent*, a word also used in grammar lessons. The surprising connection is the word *answer*. Also, the prefix *anti-*, which we think of as meaning *against*, is a surprising connection. Think about how we use words like *affront, effrontery,* and *confront* to convey a sense of opposition.

- **ap**: This prefix denotes the concept of *away*. We see it in the scientific word *apogee*. A surprising connection may be found in the word *apology*, as in "away from power, as *–pol* means power." However, this prefix usually makes its appearance in the form of *ab-*, as in *abstract* and *absolute*.

- **co, com,** and **con**: This, the most productive prefix on the list, means *with*. We have all of the math words beginning with *co-*: *coordinate, cofactor, coefficient, coaxial, collinear, cotangent, coterminal*. And we have those with *com* that are already known: *compare, compass, complex, common, complete, combine, compute/computer*. Then we have those that might be known: *compress,* *compose/composite/ composition/component, compatible.* Linking the familiar to the new, we can learn *commutative* in a way that connects it to its relatives. Using the same layout for *con*, we have the familiar words: *connect, contain, contact, construct, control, continue/continuous* to *consecutive, contradict, consequent, converse, convex, concave, converge/convergence/convergent, concordant, contour, conform, congruent.* Finally, we have our *cor*, as in the familiar *correct* to the new *correlate/correlation*. Even the most basic of math words—*count, cost, couple*—belong to this huge family.

- **de:** To mean *down*, de- appears in a substantial number of math words that are also used in general discourse. We have *degrade, decrease, denominator, dependent, depreciate, determine, degree.* A close relative is di- meaning *away*, as in *divide, dimension, diverge.* And then there's *dis-: dissect, distribute, distance, discrete, disperse.*

- **dia:** This one means through or across, as in *diagonal, diagram, diameter.*

- **The prefixes and combining forms meaning two:** I couldn't resist including these here even though they denote numbers. But there are so many, and they have morphed so much over the history of Indo-European languages, I have to mention them: The original root, *dwo-*, not seen in English anymore, now appears as *two*. It has morphed into *twin, between, twelve, twine.* It masquerades as *duplicate, double, dyad, dual, due, dichotomy.* But arguably its most common incarnation in math language is as *bi-: bisect, bimodal, binary, binomial, bipolar, bifurcate.*

- **ex:** Meaning *out*, often seen as *e-*, we find *enumerate, evaluate, exact, exceed, except, excess, exchange, exclude, expand, explicit, extract, extraneous, extreme, extrapolate, exponent.* In common language, we have *exit, exist, example, explain.*

- **iso:** Found so frequently in the math world, *iso-* means, and is related to, *equal*. Hence, *isometric, isosceles, isotope.* In common language, we find a class of words having do to not with equality, but with singularity: *isolate, island*, etc.

- **semi:** Sometimes appearing as *hemi* (*hemisphere*), *semi* means *half*, as in *semicircle*.

The Combining Forms

- **arith**: Meaning "fit together," this is the basis for the word *arithmetic*, and yields other related words, including *logarithm* and even *rhythm* and *rhyme*.

- **fer**: This very widely used word root means *to carry* or *to bear*. We see it in math words such as *circumference*, everyday words that are often used in math such as *differ, difference, differential, differentiate, infer, inference, inferential, refer, reference, referential, transfer,* and *transference*. We also see it in everyday words not usually part of the math world such as *confer, conference, conferring, prefer, preference, preferring,* and *suffer*.

- **fract**: Meaning *to break*, we see this in *fraction, fracture, fractal*. Historically, the word *break* comes from this same family, although the only remnant of that family tie is the *k* sound.

- **en**: Meaning *in*, often seen as *in-* and *im-*, we find *coincide, coincident, implicit, index, indicate, invert, parenthesize, inference*. In common language, we have *in, inner, interest, inside, envelope*.

- **fin**: Meaning *boundary*, we find *finite, infinite, infinity, infinitesimal, define, definitive*. Learning this etymology affords a good opportunity to teach the difference and similarity between the word *define* as used in math and as used in general conversation, where it means to *give the meaning of a word or term*.

- **geo**: *Geo*, of course, means Earth, as in *geography* and *geology*. When we think of *geo*, we think of maps and rocks. What about *geometry*, which does not mean "measurement of the Earth"—or does it? By asking students to connect these words, we may unfold grand insights about what geometry is really all about.

- **gon**: Now meaning *form*, the ancestor of such words as *hexagon, pentagon, octagon, polygon,* etc., is actually *genu-*, meaning *angle* and/or *knee*. In English class, the students learn the word *protagonist* for the main character in a story. Etymologically, the protagonist is the person who "forms" (*gon*) the story by moving it forward (*pro*).

- **gram** and **graph**: Originally meaning *scratch*, words with these forms denote something "scratched" onto a surface that will allow them to convey meaning.

- **kad, cid, cas,** and **cata**: We see the component *–cid*, meaning *to fall* or *by chance* in numerous common words, including *accident,* *incident, coincidence,* and *decide.* As nouns, this combining form morphs into *–cis,* as in *decision, precision, excision, incision.* We also see it in the *–cide* words that refer to killing (*insecticide, homicide, suicide, fratricide,* etc.) Mathematically, we have the words *case,* meaning, literally, *that which has fallen,* and *category/categorical,* meaning *something thrown down.* The connections here may seem farfetched, but by calling a family reunion, we can derive a common ancestry that illuminates meaning.

- **cap, cep, cept, ceive,** and **cip**: This form, meaning *to grasp,* is seen in common words such as *receive, deceive, conceive.* These words, of course, correspond to *reception, deception, conception.* Also in the family are *accept, except, intercept.* Even *principal* and *principle* are family members, as is *capacity.*

- **cess** and **ceed**: Meaning *to go* or *to yield.* Students know the words *succeed* and *success.* They use these words in ordinary conversation all the time. In social studies, they may learn the word *successor,* line of *succession* and *successor.* And in math, they hear of *successive* numbers. In both math and grammar, we speak of *antecedents* (that which goes before). Other familiar words in this family are *necessary, exceed/excess, proceed/process, recede, recess, recession.*

- **cre**: This one, as seen in *increase/increment/incremental, decrease,* and *accrue,* means *grow.*

- **cur**: Meaning *to run,* we see this one in *current, recurrent, recursive, occur/occurrence, incur.*

- **clu** and **clos**: Related to the words *close* and *closet,* this combining form actually refers to a *hook* or *peg.* So we have *conclude/conclusive/conclusion; include/inclusive/inclusion; exclude/exclusion/exclusive.*

- **syn** and **sym**: Meaning *with* or *together,* we find this combining form in many subjects: *symphony, sympathy, symbol, synthetic, symptom.* Even the word *system* is a cousin in the *syn/sym* family. In math, we have *symmetry* (together + measure) and *asymmetry* (not + together + measure).

- **qu**: The letter Q, ordinarily a shy creature, gets a workout in math class. We have *quantity/ quantify, quality/qualify/qualification, quotient.* All of these words are offspring of the word *question.*

- **lat**: If you ask students to tell you what it means in the gym when they "work their lats," they will probably know. They have learned about *latitude* and *longitude* in social studies class. In math, they meet *lateral, unilateral, bilateral trilateral, quadrilateral, equilateral*. The common meaning is *side*. A bilateral agreement, then would be an agreement reached by both sides, as opposed to a unilateral "agreement," which is actually a contradiction in terms, as you can't have an agreement by one side only. You might engage students in a conversation about bilateral and unilateral "agreements" between themselves and their friends and parents.

- **lin**: Students know what a line is, but may not make the connection to *linear*, a word that is not used much in ordinary conversation but that is essential for mathematical learning.

- **map**: Although students know the word *map*, it might be interesting for them to consider that map comes from the Indo-European word for *cloth*, and that it is also related to the word *napkin*, literally, *little cloth*.

- **me, met,** and **metr**: Another huge math word family, this combining form, unsurprisingly, means *measure*, and the word *measure* is, of course, a member of this family. From it, we get all our words that end with *–meter*, plus the words that spring from *–metry*. Geometry, then, would derive from *geo* (earth) + *metry* (measurement). *Trigonometry* would be a combination of *tri* (three) + *gon* (form) + *metry* (measurement). You might be surprised to know that the words *moon* and *month* are cousins.

- **med**: Meaning *take appropriate measures*, we find this form in *median, medial, intermediate*. Cousins are *mode, model, mean*, and all the words beginning with *meta*.

- **mag, meg, max,** and **maj**: Meaning *great*, this combining form is seen in conversational expressions like *to the max*, a shortened form of *maximum, major, majesty, majestic*. In science, we have *magnitude*. In math, *mega-* is a prefix meaning *million*. The last letter of the Greek alphabet, *omega*, is a member of this family. Closely related to this combining form is *mult*, also meaning *great*, as in all of the forms of *multiple*, including *multiply* and the prefix *multi-*.

- **min**: The opposite of the above form, *min* appears in many common words such as *minute, minimum, diminish, minor*. You can help students make the connection to minus, minimum, and the less familiar word *minuend*.

- nom and num: If you knew just a handful of words in Spanish, you would probably know that *nombre* means *name*. Accordingly, *denominator, polynomial, binomiall,* and even *number* plus its derivatives *numeration, enumerate, numerator,* are members of this family.

- ple, plic, and plex: Meaning *fold*, we have *complex/complicate, duplex/duplicate,* and the words ending with *–ple* such as *multiple, triple, quadruple*. Even the word *simple* is a member of this family as is *double*.

- per and par: Meaning *through* or *around*, this is a productive family whose members frequent all phases of math language: *perimeter, parameter, parallel, permutation, percent, parabola, paradigm*. Students may know the words *paraprofessional* or *paralegal*. They know *perfume, perfect, separate*.

- rad: Students know what a *radio* is (though I wouldn't count on them knowing this word for much longer!) and what a *ray* is. Meaning *rod*, the related words are *radial, radius, radiate, radical*.

- sec and sect: Meaning *cut*, we have *section, intersection, bisect, bisector*.

- sta: Meaning *stand*, this root is a staple for mathematical language. In fact, *staple* is one of its forms. Words having to do with *stability* (another example) often come out of this family: *constant, instant, distant, equidistant, standard, state, stationary, statistic, stem*. A chameleon form of *sta* is *sis*: *persistent, consistent,* even *system*.

- ul: This little syllable denotes the *concept of smallness* but is also used to mean *part of*. It's a wily one, appearing in *regular, circular, module/modular, singular*. We also see remnants of it in *angle, model, single, circle,* and *couple*.

The Suffixes

- nd: Many words in the math world end with *–nd*: *dividend, addend, minuend, multiplicand*. Its meaning is hard to explain in English, but I'll try. It refers to something that is to be acted upon. Thus, an *addend* is a number that is about to be added to; a *subtrahend* is the number that is about to be subtracted from the *minuend*.

The Roots

- **sin:** Not to be confused with the word *sign*, the root *sin*—as in *sine* and *cosine*—means *hollow*, *bend*, or *curve*.

- **scend:** Meaning *climb*, we see this root in the words *ascend* (*ascending*, *ascendant*) and *descend* (*descending*, *descendant*). The root also makes a slightly different appearance in the word *scale*.

- **tag, tact,** and **teg:** Meaning *touch*, we have *tangent, integer, integral, contact, integrate*.

- **term:** We think of this root as meaning *end*, and though it is often used in words having to do with endings, its true meaning is *boundary*. We have *terminal, terminate, terminating, terminology, term, determine*.

- **tract:** Meaning *draw* or *drag*, students are introduced to this word in the math world with *subtract*: literally, "drawn under" which is exactly what we do with the subtrahend when we write a subtraction problem. A familiar word in this family is *tractor*. Students will also encounter the word *protractor* in their math lives. The words *attract* and *retract* are probably familiar members of this family.

- **ver/vers:** Meaning *turn*, we see this root in many math words: *converse, inverse,* and *reverse,* and their verb forms: *convert, invert, revert*. We also find *transversal* and *traverse*.

APPENDIX 2

Making Connections in Vocabulary

Academic vocabulary acquisition would be so much easier if students understood how words are connected through common Latin and Greek roots.

cede, ceed, cess: to go, to yield
As used in math: exceed, successive

accede, access,
concede, concession
exceed, excessive
necessary, necessitate
process, procession
recede, recession,
secession, succession

clud, clus, clos: to close
As used in math: include, including inclusive, exclude, excluding, exclusive

clause
cloister
closet
conclude, conclusion
enclose
exclude, exclusion
include, inclusion
occlude, occlusion
preclude, preclusion
recluse, reclusive
seclude, seclusion

cur, curs: to run
As used in math: recurrent

current, currency
cursive
cursor
cursory
discursive
incur, incursion
occur, occurrence
recur, recursive, recurrent

♦ 111

duct, duce: to lead, to pull
As used in math: deduction, product, reduce

abduct, abductor, abduction
aqueduct
conduct
duct, ductile
deduce, deduct, deduction
induce, induct, inducement, induction
produce, product, producer, productive
reduce, reductive
seduce, seduction, seductive
transducer

fac, fic: to do, to make
As used in math: factor, factorization

de facto
faction
fact, factor
factory
fiction, fictitious
manufacture

fer, phor: to carry
As used in math: differential

confer, conference
conifer
defer, deference, deferential
differ, difference, different, differential, differentiate
infer, inference, inferential
metaphor, metaphorical
offer
phosphorescence
refer, reference, referent
suffer, sufferance, insufferable
transfer, transference

gress, grad: to step
As used in math: regression, grade, gradient

aggression, aggressive
congress, congressional
degrade
egress
grade, gradient
graduate
ingress
progress, progressive, progression
regress, regressive, regression
retrograde

ject: to throw
As used in math: trajectory

adjective
abject
deject, dejection
inject, injection
object, objective, objectify
subject, subjective
trajectory

lat: side
As used in math: lateral, bilateral, equilateral

lateral, bilateral, unilateral
latitude
relate, relative, relationship

mit, miss: to send
As used in math: omit, omission

Admit, admission
remit, emit, omit, transmit, admission, permission, remission, emission, omission, transmission, mission, missionary, submit, submissive, submission

nom, nym: to name
As used in math: denominator, polynomial, binomial

nominate, denominator, nominal, ignominy, nomenclature, synonym, acronym, homonym, polynomial, binomial

plic, plex: to fold
As used in math: duplicate, replicate

complicate, complicit, implicate, explicate, explicit, implicit
accomplice, supplicate, duplicate, replicate
complex

reg, rect: straight
As used in math: rectangle, regular

rectangle, regular, rectify, erect, rectitude, correct, direct

script, scribe: write

transcript, scripture, conscription, prescription, subscription, prescribe, transcribe, subscribe, proscribe, inscribe, inscription, describe, description, manuscript

sect, sec: to cut
As used in math: section, bisector, transect, intersect

section, secular, bisect, dissect, intersect, transect, sector, secant

Making Connections in Vocabulary ♦ 113

ten, tin, tain, tang, tex, tec, tac, teg:
to touch, to hold
As used in math: tangent

ascertain
attack
attain
attend, attention
contain, containment
contend, contention
contingent, contingency
detain, detention, detainee
extend, extensive, extension
integer, integral, integrity, intact
intend, intensive, intention
maintain, maintenance
pretend, pretense, pretension
pretext
retain, retention
sustain, sustenance
tactile, tacky, tact, texture
tenure, tenant, tenet,
texture, text, tangential

tract: to drag, to draw
As used in math: subtract, extract

attract, attractive, attraction
contract, contraction
detract
distract, distraction
extract, extraction
intractable
protract, protractor, protracted
retract, retraction
subtract, subtraction
traction, tractor, tractable

vert, vers: to turn
As used in math: inverse, obverse,
reverse, converse

averse, aversion, avert
adversity
converse, controversy, convert, conversion
diverse, diversion, divert
inverse, inversion
obverse
reverse, reversion, revert
subvert, subversive, subversion
versatile, verse

Works Cited

Achieve. (2010, August). *Comparing the common core state standards and Japan's mathematics curriculum in the course of study.* Retrieved from http://www.achieve.org/files/CCSSandJapan.pdf

America's perfect storm: three forces changing our nation's future—New Jersey's challenge. (2007, April 18). PEI Roundtable cosponsored by the Educational Testing Service and the Public Education Institute. Retrieved from http://cesp.rutgers.edu/PEI/Resources/PEI-041807-summary.pdf.

Bangert-Drowns, R. L., Hurley, M. M., & Wilkenson, B. (2007). How does writing affect learning? A review of the research. Retrieved from http://www.csun.edu/~krowlands/Content/Academic_Resources/Composition/Tool%20for%20Learning/How%20Writing%20Affects%20Learning_files/howdoes.htm

Basic number properties: distributive, associative, commutative. (n.d.). Retrieved from http://www.purplemath.com/mudules/numbprop.htm.

Big ideas in beginning reading: vocabulary, concepts and research. (n.d.). Retrieved April, 2011 from http://reading.uroregon.edu/big_ideas/voc/voc_what.php.

Bossenbroek, J. (n.d.). Define, compare, contrast, explain... Retrieved from http://www.maa.org/saum/maanotes49/104.html.

Burns, M. (2008). *Problem-solving lessons.* Sausalito, CA: Math Solutions.

Carrafiello, J. (1997). *Pre-algebra.* Upper Saddle River, NJ: Globe Fearon.

Cavanagh, M. C. (2000). *Math to know. A mathematics handbook.* Boston: Great Source Education Group.

Chui, M. M. (2000, Summer). Metaphorical reasoning: origins, uses, development and interactions in mathematics. *Education Journal, 28*(1), 13–46. Retrieved from http://www.fed.cuhk.edu.hk/staff/paper/mmchiu/02-03/m4theory.pdf.

Common core state standards initiative. (2010). Retrieved from http://www.corestandards. org.

Concept-rich mathematics instruction. (n.d.). Retrieved from http://www.ascd.org/publications/books/106008/chapters/Conceptual_Understanding.aspx.

Cook, S. W., & Goldin-Meadow, S. (2006). The role of gesture in learning: do children use their hands to change their minds? *Journal of Cognition and Development, 7*(2), 211–232.

Coxhead, A. (2000). A new academic word list. *TESOL Quarterly, 34,* 213–238.

de Klerk, J. (1999). *Illustrated math dictionary: an essential student resource.* Parsippany, NJ: Globe Fearon.

Freemen, M. (1986). *Creative graphing.* New Rochelle, NY: Cuisenaire Company of America.

Freitag, M. (1998, Winter). Reading and writing in the mathematics classroom. *The Mathematics Educator, 8*(1).

Fuentes, P. (1998, November-December). Reading comprehension in mathematics. *Heldref Publications, 72*(2), 81–88.

Gantert, A. X. (2007). *Integrated algebra.* New York: Amsco.

Geometry test sampler. (2008). Retrieved from http:/www.emsc.nysed.gov/osa/mathre/geometry-sampler.pdf.

Graff, L., Culhan, D., & Marhuenda-Donate, F. (2006). Outlining mathematics. Retrieved from http://www.cfkeep.org/html/stitch.php?s=14832740290866&id=34947815104339.

Heath, C., & Heath, D. (2007, 2008). *Made to stick: why some ideas survive and others die.* New York: Random House.

Hyde, A. (2006). *Comprehending math: adapting reading strategies to teach mathematics, K-6.* Portsmouth, NH: Heinemann.

Jacobs, H. H. (2006). *Active literacy across the curriculum: strategies for reading, writing, speaking, and listening.* Larchmont, NY: Eye On Education.

Just what is algebraic thinking? (n.d.). Retrieved from http://www.emse.nysed.gov/osa/mathre/grometry-sampler.pdf.

Kenney, J. M., Hancewitz, E., Heuer, L., Metsisto, D., & Tuttle, C. L. (2005). *Literacy strategies for improving mathematics instruction.* Alexandria, VA: ASCD.

Krashen, S. D. (1981). Theory of second language acquisition. Retrieved from http://www.sdkrashen.com/SL_Acquisition_and_Learning/index.html

Krashen, S. D. (2004). *The power of reading: insights from the research.* Portsmouth, NH: Heinemann.

Language cards: photos for developing oral and written language skills. (2004). Grand Rapids, MI: North Star Teacher Resources.

Larwin, K. H. (2010, October). Reading is fundamental for predicting math achievement in 10th graders. *International Electronic Journal of Mathematics Education, 5*(3), 133–143.

Math lessons. (n.d.). Retrieved from http://www.math-lessons.ca/blog/.

Merlino, F. J. (n.d.). Understanding integrated mathematics using living metaphors. Retrieved from http://www.nctm.org/resources/countent/aspx?id-1674.

Molina, C. (2010, July). *The trouble with math is English.* Presentation at the Conference for the Advancement of Mathematics Teaching, San Antonio,

TX. Retrieved from http://www.sedl.org/presentations/0001/the-trouble-with-math-is-english.pdf.

Muschla, J. A., & Robert, G. (1995). *The math teacher's book of lists.* Englewood Cliffs, NJ: Prentice Hall.

NCTM. (n.d.). Lessons and teaching. Retrieved from http://my.nctm.org/resources/content.aspx?id=16385.

NCTM. (n.d.). Table of standards. http://standards.nctm.org/document/appendix/alg.htm.

Neil, M. S. (1996). *Mathematics the write way: activities for every elementary classroom.* Larchmont, NY: Eye On Education.

New York State Education Department. (2007). Mathematics test: grade 7, books 1 and 2; grade 8, books 1, 2, and 3. Albany, NY: Author.

New York State Education Department. (n.d.) Suggested list of mathematical Language. Albany, NY: Author.

New York State learning standards. (n.d.). Retrieved from http://www.thinkfinity.org/NYSS_Math.php.

New York State learning standards. Grade 5. (n.d.). Retrieved from http://www.thinkfinityny.org/standards_math.php?GRADEDESC=Grade+5.

North Carolina Department of Public Instruction. (2003). *Mathematics standard course of study: purpose.* Retrieved from http://www.ncpublicschools.org/curriculum/mathematics/scos/2003/intro/06purpose?&print=true

Parameswaran, R. (2010). Expert mathematicians' approach to understanding definition. *The Mathematics Educator, 20*(1), 43–51.

Pecchioni, F. (2001). English grammar—in math class? Oh, yes. *NADE Selected Conference Papers, vol. 7.*

Polya, G. (1957). *The four-step problem-solving process.* Retrieved from http://www.drkhamsi.com/classe/polya.html.

Sadler, F. H. (2009). Help! They still don't understand counting. *Teaching Exceptional Children Plus, 6*(1), 1–11.

Schwartzman, S. (1994). *The words of mathematics: an etymological dictionary of mathematical terms used in English.* Washington, DC: The Mathematical Association of America.

Seeley, C. (2006). Teaching to the test. From The President's Corner of the National Council of Teachers of Mathematics. Retrieved from http://www.nctm.org.

Standards for Mathematical Practice. (2010). *Common core state standards initiative.* Retrieved from http://www.corestandards.org/the-standards/mathematics/introduction/standards-for-mathematical-practice/.

Sousa, D. A. (2008). *How the brain learns mathematics.* Thousand Oaks, CA: Corwin.

Tate, M. L. (2009). *Mathematics worksheets don't grow dendrites: numeracy strategies that engage the brain, preK-8*. Thousand Oaks, CA: Corwin.

Teaching gap exists among US and Asian math teachers, study says. (2007, May 5). Retrieved from http://www.sciencedaily.com/releases/2007/05/0705241053.htm.

The role of gesture in learning: do children use their hands to change their minds? (n.d.). Retrieved from http://www.psychology.uiowa.edu/faculty/cook/Resources/06JCDCookGM.pdf.

Thiessen, D., ed. (2004). *Exploring mathematics through literature*. Reston: NCTM.

Twomey Fosnot, C., & Dolk, M. (2002). *Young mathematicians at work: constructing fractions, decimals, and percents*. Portsmouth, NH: Heinemann.

Twomey Fosnot, C., & Dolk, M. (2002). *Young mathematicians at work: constructing multiplication and division*. Portsmouth, NH: Heinemann.

Twomey Fosnot, C., & Dolk, M. (2002). *Young mathematicians at work: constructing number sense, addition, and subtraction*. Portsmouth, NH: Heinemann.

Whitin, D., & Whitin, P. (2000). *Math is language too*. Urbana, IL: NCTE.

Whitin, D. J., & Whitin, P. (2004). *New visions for linking literature and mathematics*. Urbana, IL: NCTE.

Wiliam, D. (n.d.). Keeping learning on track: formative assessment and the regulation of learning. Learning and Teaching Research Center. Educational Testing Service. Delivered at the Twentieth Biennial Conference of the Australian Association of Mathematics Teachers.

Zhihui, F., & Schleppergrell, M. J. (2010, April 11). Disciplinary literacies across content areas: supporting secondary reading through functional language analysis. *Journal of Adolescent & Adult Literacy, 53*(7), 587–597.

Zike, K. (2003). *Big book of math*. San Antonio, TX: DMA.